Study Guide to Accompany
ADJUSTMENT AND GROWTH IN A CHANGING WORLD

Prepared by

Vince Napoli
Miami Dade Community College, South Campus

James M. Kilbride
Miami Dade Community College, South Campus

Donald E. Tebbs
Miami Dade Community College, South Campus

D1212420

WEST PUBLISHING COMPANY
St. Paul   New York   Los Angeles   San Francisco

Copyright © 1982 by   WEST PUBLISHING COMPANY
                      50 West Kellogg Boulevard
                      P.O. Box 3526
                      St. Paul, Minnesota 55165

Printed in the United States of America
ISBN # 0-314-63281-6

CONTENTS

INTRODUCTION

This <u>Study Guide</u> has been prepared to help you learn the major concepts presented in <u>Adjustment and Growth in a Changing World</u>. Its design is straight-forward and simple and, if you complete the specified tasks, you will learn the concepts well.

Each chapter in this <u>Guide</u> is divided into six sections:

CHAPTER TERMS AND CONCEPTS--This section is a listing of twenty terms and con-cepts that are essential to an understanding of the material presented in the corresponding chapter in <u>Adjustment and Growth in a Changing World</u>. Its purpose is to focus your attention on the major ideas presented in that chapter.

BEHAVIORAL OBJECTIVES--This section is a listing of a few of the important goals you will achieve by learning the major concepts. Its purpose is to focus your attention on what you will be able to do when you master the concepts.

SEARCH FOR MEANING--This section consists of several incomplete statements and/or questions that are based on the major concepts. Its purpose is to require you to read the chapter thoroughly so that you will understand the con-cepts.

PERSONAL SYNTHESIS--This section consists of one or more broadly based "think" questions, the answers to which require your own personal perspective. Its purpose is to require you to apply the major concepts in the construction of your answers.

SELF QUIZ--This section consists of two ten-question quizzes that are based on the major concepts. One of the quizzes is "True or False;" the other is "Fill in the Blanks." The purpose of this section is to test your understanding of the concepts.

ANSWERS TO QUIZZES--This section is a listing of correct answers to the quiz questions, including number references to similar questions in the "Review Questions" section of the corresponding chapter in <u>Adjustment and Growth in a Changing World</u>. Its purpose is to verify your understanding of the major con-cepts.

As we have indicated, if you complete the specified tasks, you will learn the concepts well. Good luck!

V. N.
J. M. K.
D. E. T.

PART ONE THE INDIVIDUAL AND SOCIETY

Chapter
ONE

Personality

CHAPTER TERMS AND CONCEPTS

The following terms and concepts are considered essential to an understanding of the material presented in Chapter 1, "Personality."

1. personality
2. traits and types
3. personality model
4. psychoanalysis
5. personality structure
6. levels of mental awareness
7. defense
8. fixation
9. stages of development
10. respondent conditioning
11. behaviorism
12. operant conditioning
13. reinforcement
14. reinforcement schedules
15. law of effect
16. humanism
17. actualization drive
18. conditional positive regard
19. voluntary growth
20. congruence

BEHAVIORAL OBJECTIVES

After reading and reflecting on the material presented in Chapter 1, "Personality," you should be able to:

1. define personality and identify the two major ways psychologists describe personality;

2. identify the characteristics of each of the three approaches to personality presented in the chapter;

3. compare and contrast the three personality models presented in the chapter.

SEARCH FOR MEANING

Complete the following statements after locating the appropriate information as it appears in Chapter 1.

1. Most psychologists agree on at least three characteristics of <u>personality</u>. They are:

    a. _____

    _____

    b. _____

    _____

    c. _____

    _____

2. Psychologists, as well as most of us, describe personality in what two ways?

    a. _____

    b. _____

3. Psychologists often refer to <u>personality models</u> in their attempts to describe the personalities of specific individuals. What is a personality model, and how may it be used?

    _____

    _____

    _____

    _____

    _____

4. Sigmund Freud's system of psychological thought includes:

    a. _____

    b. _____

5. Frued identifies three structural components of personality. Name and describe each of them:

a. _____

_____

b. _____

_____

c. _____

_____

6. Freud views the mind as operating on three different levels. Name and describe each of them:

a. _____

_____

b. _____

_____

c. _____

_____

7. According to Freud, the only way to reduce tension from both the id and the superego simultaneously is through the process of <u>defense</u>. Define defense and write a brief example of defensive functioning:

_____

_____

_____

_____

_____

_____

8. According to Freud, a person may become <u>fixated</u> at some point in his or her psychological development by being either too indulged or too frustrated. What is a fixation and when may fixations occur? Give an example:

_____

_____

_____

_____

_____

_____

9. Freud identifies five psychosexual stages of development. Name each of
    these stages and its identifying characteristics:

    a. _____

        _____

    b. _____

        _____

    c. _____

        _____

    d. _____

        _____

    e. _____

        _____

10. Define respondent conditioning and give two examples of it:

    _____

    _____

    _____

    _____

    _____

11. Define behaviorism:

    _____

    _____

    _____

12. Define operant conditioning and give two examples of it:

    _____

_____

_____

_____

_____

13. Define <u>reinforcement</u> and explain the difference between <u>positive</u> <u>reinforcement</u> and <u>negative reinforcement</u>. Give an example of each:

_____

_____

_____

_____

_____

_____

14. Provide a definition and an example for each of the following <u>reinforcement</u> <u>schedules</u>:

   a. fixed-interval schedule _____

   _____

   _____

   b. variable-interval schedule _____

   _____

   _____

   c. fixed-ratio schedule _____

   _____

   _____

   d. variable-ratio schedule _____

   _____

   _____

15. State the <u>law</u> <u>of</u> effect:

_____

_____

_____

16. How do <u>humanists</u> differ from both behaviorists and psychoanalysts in
    their approach to individual behavior?

    _____

    _____

    _____

    _____

    _____

17. Compare and contrast Freud's self-preservation drive with Rogers'
    <u>actualization</u> <u>drive</u>:

    _____

    _____

    _____

    _____

    _____

18. What is <u>conditional</u> <u>positive</u> <u>regard</u> and why does Rogers believe it is such
    a debilitating factor in personality development?

    _____

    _____

    _____

    _____

19. Give three examples of your own <u>voluntary</u> <u>growth</u>:

    a. _____

       _____

    b. _____

       _____

c. _____

_____

20. Define the following two terms and provide an example for each from your own personal past.

a. <u>incongruence</u>: _____

_____

_____

b. <u>congruence</u>: _____

_____

_____

PERSONAL SYNTHESIS

Reflect for a few minutes on the "Who Am I?" essay you wrote in the last section of the Self Management for Chapter 1 in your textbook. This should help to bring into focus many of the facets of your personality.

Now, using as many of the terms and concepts from Chapter 1 as you can, write an analysis of your personality from the standpoint of each of the three personality models presented in the chapter. Try to be specific, and use examples wherever possible.

_____

_____

_____

_____

_____

_____

_____

_____

_____

_____

_____

SELF QUIZ

True or False

1. _____ The term personality involves a person's pattern of thoughts, feelings, and actions.

2. _____ Traits and types are used by psychologists as well as by most of us to describe personality.

3. _____ We can refer to what a personality is and how it works by using a personality structure.

4. _____ Psychoanalysis was founded by Sigmund Freud.

5. _____ Freud views the id, ego, and superego as the three structural components of personality.

6. _____ According to Freud, the mind operates on two levels: the unconscious and the conscious.

7. _____ When we offer reasonable and acceptable explanations for un-reasonable and unacceptable behavior, we are using rationalization.

8. _____ An individual can become fixated in only one of the three psychosexual stages.

9. _____ According to Freud, the sexual drive is temporarily inactive during the latency stage.

10. _____ Respondent conditioning is a kind of learning in which an emitted behavior produces consequences so that the probability that the behavior will be repeated under similar circumstances in the future is changed.

Fill in the Blanks

11. Psychologists who focus on observable behavior and on the observable conditions that may cause behavior are called b_____.

12. In operant conditioning, the stimulus always f_____ the response.

13. P_____ r_____ occurs when something perceived as pleasant follows a response.

14. A fixed-interval schedule of reinforcement occurs when the time between reinforcers is c_____.

15. The l_____ of e_____ states that responses that lead to satisfying consequences are strengthened and therefore tend to be repeated, and responses that lead to unsatisfying consequences are weakened and therefore tend not to be repeated.

16. Scholars who view humans as having free choice of and responsibility for their own behavior are called h_____.

17. Our biological tendency to become what we can become is known as the a_____ d_____.

18. A person who receives only partial acceptance, support, and respect from people who are important to him or her receives c_____ p_____ r_____.

19. A fulfillment theorist would view your conscious decision to become better educated by going to college as an expression of v_____ g_____.

20. When we restrict the full expression of our potentialities, we are in a state of i_____.

Answers and Question Numbers in REVIEW QUESTIONS section of chapter.

1. True (1)

2. True (3)

3. False (6)

4. True (9)

5. True (8)

6. False (8, 10)

7. True (10)

8. False (11)

9. True (11, 12)

10. False (14, 15)

11. behaviorists (13)

12. follows (15)

13. Positive reinforcement (16)

14. constant (17)

15. law of effect (20)

16. humanists (22)

17. actualization drive (23)

18. conditional positive regard (25)

19. voluntary growth (23)

20. incongruence (26)

Chapter
TWO

Socialization

CHAPTER TERMS AND CONCEPTS

The following terms and concepts are considered essential to an understanding of the material presented in Chapter 2, "Socialization."

1. socialization
2. culture
3. heredity
4. physical development
5. cognitive maturation
6. social development
7. social statuses and roles
8. human nature
9. primary groups
10. critical period
11. physiological needs
12. psychological needs
13. psychological development
14. self
15. social norms
16. beliefs
17. stereotype
18. values
19. agencies of socialization
20. life cycle

BEHAVIORAL OBJECTIVES

After reading and reflecting on the material presented in Chapter 2, "Socialization," you should be able to:

1. define socialization and explain how both hereditary and environmental factors contribute to the process of socialization;

2. list prominent human physiological and psychological needs, and discuss how the fulfillment of these needs contributes to the normal development of a person;

3. define self and discuss the impact of beliefs, stereotypes, and values on self-development;

4. list important agencies of socialization and describe how these agencies contribute to the socialization process;

12

5. define <u>life cycle</u> and compare and contrast Freud's conception of the life cycle with that of Erik Erikson.

SEARCH FOR MEANING

Complete the following statements after locating the appropriate information as it appears in Chapter 2.

1. What is <u>socialization</u>?

_____

_____

2. Define <u>culture</u> and explain why its transmission is critically important:

_____

_____

_____

_____

_____

_____

3. Both <u>heredity</u> and <u>environment</u> contribute to the socialization process. Which is the stronger influence on a person's development? Explain your answer:

_____

_____

_____

_____

_____

_____

_____

_____

_____

4. Define <u>physical</u> <u>development</u> and give three examples of it:

   _____

   _____

   a. _____

   _____

   b. _____

   _____

   c. _____

   _____

5. Define <u>cognitive</u> <u>maturation</u> and describe the usual pattern of cognitive maturation during infancy:

   _____

   _____

   _____

   _____

   _____

   _____

6. What is <u>social</u> <u>development</u>? Describe the general sequence of social development:

   _____

   _____

   _____

   _____

7. Define <u>social</u> <u>status</u> and <u>social</u> <u>role</u> and explain the relationship between them:

   _____

   _____

_____

_____

_____

_____

8. <u>Human</u> <u>nature</u> means different things to different people. Provide the
    definition for human nature associated with each of the following
    scholars.

    a. Sigmund Freud: _____

        _____

    b. B. F. Skinner: _____

        _____

    c. Carl Rogers: _____

        _____

    d. Frederick Elkin: _____

        _____

    Explain Elkin's view on how human nature develops:

    _____

    _____

    _____

    _____

    _____

9. What is a <u>primary</u> <u>group</u>?

    _____

    _____

    Give an example of a primary group:

    _____

10. Describe the "<u>critical</u> <u>periods</u> <u>hypothesis</u>."

    _____

_____

_____

_____

_____

11. What is a <u>physiological</u> <u>need</u>?

_____

_____

_____

Give three examples of physiological needs:

a. _____

b. _____

c. _____

12. What is a <u>psychological</u> <u>need</u>?

_____

_____

Give four examples of psychological needs:

a. _____

b. _____

c. _____

d. _____

Explain Maslow's hierarchy of needs:

_____

_____

_____

_____

_____

_____

_____

_____

_____

13. What is <u>psychological</u> <u>development</u>?

_____

_____

14. What is the <u>self</u>?

_____

_____

_____

Describe G. H. Mead's view of self-development:

_____

_____

_____

_____

_____

_____

_____

_____

15. What are <u>social</u> <u>norms</u>?

_____

_____

What is the relationship between the internalization of social norms and self-development?

_____

_____

_____

_____

_____

16. What is a <u>belief</u>?

_____

_____

How are beliefs formed?

_____

_____

_____

_____

_____

_____

_____

17. What is a <u>stereotype</u>?

_____

_____

Are stereotypes ever functional? _____ Explain your answer:

_____

_____

_____

_____

Are stereotypes ever dysfunctional? _____ Explain your answer:

_____

_____

_____

_____

_____

18. What is a value?

_____

_____

How is it possible for one person's value to be another's evaluative
belief?

_____

_____

_____

_____

What is value conflict and how may a value conflict be resolved?

_____

_____

_____

_____

_____

19. What is an agency of socialization?

_____

_____

List seven important agencies, and briefly describe how each contributes
to the socialization process:

a. _____

    _____

    _____

b. _____

_____

_____

c. _____

_____

_____

d. _____

_____

_____

e. _____

_____

_____

f. _____

_____

_____

g. _____

_____

_____

20. What is the _life_ _cycle_?

_____

_____

Compare and contrast Freud's conception of the life cycle with that of
Erik Erikson:

_____

_____

_____

_____

_____

_____

_____

_____

_____

_____

_____

_____

_____

_____

_____

_____

_____

_____

_____

_____

PERSONAL SYNTHESIS

The Self Management for Chapter 2 in your textbook is designed to help you to gain greater understanding of your emerging self by focusing on aspects of both your personal past and present functioning. Take a few minutes to read and reflect on that Self Management.

Now, using as many of the terms and concepts from Chapter 2 as you can, explain how you came to be who you are.

_____

_____

_____

_____

_____

_____

_____

SELF QUIZ

<u>True</u> or <u>False</u>

1. _____ The process by which human culture is transmitted is called <u>socialization</u>.

2. _____ <u>Culture</u> refers to the learned and shared way of life of a society, including its beliefs and values, but <u>not</u> its group habits or standards for behavior.

3. _____ <u>Heredity</u> is a much weaker influence in the socialization process than is environment.

4. _____ Human <u>physical development</u> does not begin until the fetal stage.

5. _____ <u>Cognitive maturation</u> is the unfolding of our potential to know.

6. _____ The first stage in the general sequence of <u>social development</u> is one of independence.

7. _____ In all societies social development is correlated with physical and mental development so that people are not expected to fill <u>statuses</u> and play <u>roles</u> that are beyond their physical and mental capabilities at any given time.

8. _____ There is a universally agreed upon definition of <u>human nature</u>.

9. _____ The relationship between you and your best friend is a <u>primary</u> relationship.

10. _____ There is some evidence that suggests the possibility of a <u>critical period</u> in the development of humans.

<u>Fill in the Blanks</u>

11. At the base of Abraham Maslow's hierarchy or pyramid of needs are our p_____ needs.

12. Eric Berne maintains that we have a p_____ need for symbolic strokes such as words, gestures, or looks that imply recognition.

13. A person's progression from simple to more complex levels of awareness of self and the relationship between self and society is called p_____ d_____.

14. The s_____ includes both notions of who and what we are in a physical, mental, emotional, and social sense and who and what we would like to be.

15. S_____ n_____ are society's rules and regulations.

16. B_____ are perceived relationships between two things, or between one thing and one of its characteristics.

17. When we treat a generalization as being universally true, we are engaging in the process known as s_____.

18. If you believe that loyalty is intrinsically desirable, then it would be correct to say that loyalty is one of your v_____.

19. In order to ensure that important beliefs, values, customs, and social norms are transmitted from one generation to the next, societies channel their transmission through particular social structures called a_____ o_____ s_____.

20. L_____ c_____ refers to the general sequence of events in our physical, psychological, and social development as we progress from infancy through old age.

Answers and Question Numbers in REVIEW QUESTIONS section of chapter.

1. True (7)	11. physiological (11)
2. False (1)	12. psychological (13)
3. False (2)	13. psychological development (16, 17)
4. False (3)	14. self (15)
5. True (4)	15. Social norms (18)
6. False (6)	16. Beliefs (19)
7. True (5)	17. stereotyping (20)
8. False (9)	18. values (21)
9. True (10)	19. agencies of socialization (22, 23, 24, 26)
10. True (12)	20. Life cycle (27)

Chapter
THREE

Self-Esteem

CHAPTER TERMS AND CONCEPTS

The following terms and concepts are considered essential to an understanding of the material presented in Chapter 3, "Self-Esteem."

1. self-esteem
2. ideal-self
3. real-self
4. malevolent attitude
5. shaping influences
6. positive self-esteem
7. negative self-esteem
8. self-esteem development
9. attitudes
10. behavior
11. feelings
12. self-alienation
13. authentic self-disclosure
14. self-love
15. integrity
16. irrational beliefs
17. rational beliefs
18. factors affecting self-esteem
19. negative self-statements
20. positive self-statements

BEHAVIORAL OBJECTIVES

After reading and reflecting on the material presented in Chapter 3, "Self-Esteem," you should be able to:

1. define self-esteem and understand its importance as to the way you live your life;

2. identify the characteristics of the various levels of self-esteem;

3. identify your own level of self-esteem;

4. describe how our self-esteem develops from birth into adulthood;

5. describe ways that we can maintain a positive level of self-esteem.

SEARCH FOR MEANING

Complete the following statements after locating the appropriate information as it appears in Chapter 3.

1. The ideal-self is:

    _____

    _____

2. <u>Self-esteem</u> is one of the most important parts of our self-concept. It is defined as:

    _____

    _____

3. How does Sullivan's concept of the <u>malevolent attitude</u> relate to someone's self-esteem?

    _____

    _____

    _____

4. How does guilt affect our feelings of worth?

    _____

    _____

    _____

5. What role does our "shaping influences" play in the development of our self-esteem?

    _____

    _____

6. What is meant by the statement, "Self-esteem is a process."?

    _____

    _____

    _____

7. Describe the six reasons why Berelson believes many parents have children:

a. _____

b. _____

c. _____

d. _____

e. _____

f. _____

8. List three personal factors which contribute to our self-esteem:

a. _____

b. _____

c. _____

9. What is Karen Horney referring to when she uses the word "self-alienation"?

_____

_____

10. How does Jourard suggest that we achieve and maintain a healthy personality?

_____

_____

_____

_____

11. List as many characteristics as is possible of the person with a positive self-esteem:

_____

_____

_____

_____

12. Describe the benefits Fromm suggests for loving yourself:

_____

_____

_____

_____

_____

13. Describe the association between integrity and self-esteem:

_____

_____

_____

14. List the feelings that characterize the individual with chronic low self-worth:

_____

_____

_____

15. Give three examples of what Ellis and Harper call irrational beliefs:

a. _____

b. _____

c. _____

16. How might Ellis and Harper respond to the statement, "I cannot see myself taking a French course. I could never learn to speak it well enough."?

_____

_____

_____

_____

17. How do attitudes affect our behavior?

_____

_____

_____

_____

18. Give three examples of positive self-statements:

    a. _____

    b. _____

    c. _____

19. Describe Aaron Beck's view of the relationship between thinking and behaving:

    _____

    _____

    _____

    _____

    _____

    _____

20. Explain why people seem to affect our self-worth more than any other factor:

    _____

    _____

    _____

    _____

    _____

    _____

PERSONAL SYNTHESIS

   Reflect a few moments on the learning, thoughts, and feelings you have experienced while reading Chapter 3. Using as many terms and concepts as are appropriate to you, assess your present level of self-esteem. The process of achieving a healthier self-esteem begins by being honest with yourself.

_____

_____

_____

SELF QUIZ

True or False

1. _____ It is important for a person with positive self-esteem to avoid negative experiences.

2. _____ Our self-worth is actually the result of our self-image.

3. _____ It is important to realize that the development of our self-esteem is never completed.

4. _____ Our attitudes, feelings, and behavior greatly contribute to our self-esteem.

5. _____ The person with low self-esteem is always taking risks.

6. _____ Erich Fromm believes that we cannot love others genuinely while loving ourselves.

7. _____ We are more susceptible to fear, hurt, and rejection when we are experiencing low self-esteem.

8. _____ Behavior is the result of our intelligence.

9. _____ The belief that others are going to do what they want rather than what we want is an example of helplessness.

10. _____ People probably have a greater effect on our personality than any other factor.

Fill in the Blanks

11. The _____ _____ represents those personal characteristics that we believe we should have.

12. The value we place on ourselves is referred to as our _____

_____.

13. The _____ attitude is the belief that we live among enemies.

14. _____ suggests that some of our esteem problems may be due to the reasons why we were born.

15. The state of losing contact with our real selves is defined by Karen Horney as _____ _____.

16. Sidney Jourard believes that a healthy personality can be achieved and maintained by risking authentic _____.

17. When our thoughts, feelings, and behaviors are consistent with each other we are said to have _____.

18. An _____ _____ is represented by the statement, "Everyone must like me."

19. Ellis and Harper believe that the negative interpretations we make about our life experience results from a problem with our _____.

20. The belief that we can change our thinking by changing our _____ is proposed by Aaron Beck.

Answers and Question Numbers in REVIEW QUESTIONS section of chapter.

1. False (9)   11. ideal self (4)

2. False (12, 13)   12. self-esteem (1)

3. True (15)   13. malevolent (11)

4. True (2)   14. Berelson (14)

5. False (6)   15. self-alienation (3)

6. False (10)   16. self-disclosure (2)

7. True (3)   17. integrity (8)

8. False (17)   18. irrational belief (16)

9. False (18)   19. thinking (16)

10. True (19)   20. behavior (20)

PART TWO IDENTITY IN TRANSITION

Chapter

FOUR

Physical Self

CHAPTER TERMS AND CONCEPTS

The following terms and concepts are considered essential to an understanding of the material presented in Chapter 4, "Physical Self."

 1. adaptation
 2. homeostasis
 3. somatotypes
 4. personality traits
 5. personality disorders
 6. children and body type
 7. "The Looking Glass Self"
 8. "bodily me"
 9. physical attraction
10. stigma

11. attribution theory
12. determinism
13. physical fitness
14. training goals
15. types of fitness
16. aerobics
17. obesity
18. causes of obesity
19. weight loss
20. All American Diet

BEHAVIORAL OBJECTIVES

After reading and reflecting on the material presented in Chapter 4,
"Physical Self," you should be able to:

1. define adaptation and homeostasis and relate each to the concept of the
    limits imposed by the physical self;

2. identify Sheldon's three somatotypes and match each with its correspond-
    ing cluster of personality traits;

3. describe the function of attribution theory and the importance of a
    healthy body and bodily self-concept;

4. list important aspects of physical fitness and the training procedures
    recommended for reaching fitness goals;

5. define <u>obesity</u> and describe its relationship to energy consumption and
    energy expenditure.

SEARCH FOR MEANING

    Complete the following statements after locating the appropriate infor-
mation as it appears in Chapter 4.

1. Define the physical self:

    _____

    _____

    _____

2. List several limits that our morphogenotype places on our ability to
    adjust to the demands of a changing world:

    a. _____

    b. _____

    c. _____

3. Physicians, poets, and philosophers have long noted a correlation between
    physique and character. List the three broad <u>bodily types</u> into which the
    ancients seem to divide mankind:

    a. _____

    b. _____

    c. _____

4. Name and give a brief description of the clusters of personality traits
    that Sheldon associates with each body type:

    a. _____

    b. _____

    c. _____

    What body type is most heavily represented at universities? _____

    _____

    What personality traits help this type to succeed in college? _____

    _____

_____

_____

What traits work against this type enjoying the college years to the maximum?

_____

_____

_____

5. Which somatotype is associated with juvenile delinquency? _____

_____

What reason, other than genetics, could possibly account for this type being over-represented among delinquents?

_____

_____

In which somatic populations is the greatest amount of <u>anxiety</u> found?

_____

The most depression? _____

6. What advice is given by the Gessell Institute to parents regarding bodily types of infants and successful parenting?

_____

_____

7. Define "The Looking Glass Self": _____

_____

_____

_____

What stereotypes exist in the minds of most of us concerning:

a. <u>Endomorphs</u>: _____

_____

b. <u>Mesomorphs</u>: _____

_____

c. <u>Ectomorphs</u>: _____

_____

Why does Diamond (1957) believe that we observe our own bodies and the bodies of others?

_____

_____

8. Define the "bodily me" (Allport, 1960) and list its expressed functions:

_____

_____

_____

9. How does being physically attractive affect:

a. nursery school children? _____

_____

b. criminal defendants? _____

_____

c. the elderly? _____

_____

What is the relationship between personal status and perceived height?

_____

_____

10. <u>Define stigma</u>: _____

_____

What physical characteristics are too often associated with being <u>stigmatized</u> in contemporary America?

_____

_____

_____

In what way is it unwarranted to respond to an individual in terms of a "true" stereotype?

_____

_____

What did Jane Elliott do to teach her third grade class the "irrationality" of racism?

_____

_____

What were the results of her role-playing experiment?

_____

_____

11. Define <u>attribution theory</u>: _____

_____

_____

What four statements (Nisbett) support the idea that our observations are seldom fair and impartial?

a. _____

b. _____

c. _____

d. _____

12. To what or whom do we tend to attribute our bad behavior? _____

_____

Our good behavior? _____

_____

What appears to be a severe limitation on the utility of current attribution theory?

_____

_____

13. What does it mean to be physically fit? _____

In the long run, what is the most important form of physical fitness?

_____

14. List the six goals for <u>physical</u> <u>training</u> as given by Van Huss:

    a. _____

    b. _____

    c. _____

    d. _____

    e. _____

    f. _____

15. How may repressed emotions be related to bodily posture? _____

    _____

    _____

    _____

    What must we do every day if we are to maintain a high degree of flexi-
    bility?

    _____

    _____

    What are the steps in strength training? _____

    _____

    _____

    _____

    _____

16. Define <u>aerobic</u> fitness: _____

    _____

    What must you do to achieve aerobic fitness? _____

    _____

_____

_____

17. Define <u>obesity</u>: _____

_____

In what ways are stereotypical notions of the obese founded on fact?

_____

_____

_____

Can a person be more than ten percent overweight and yet not be fat?

_____

18. What is the <u>direct</u> <u>cause</u> of obesity? _____

_____

List several indirect causes of obesity:

a. _____

b. _____

c. _____

d. _____

How are genetics and infant feeding patterns related to adult obesity?

_____

_____

_____

19. To achieve weight loss, it is necessary to:

a. _____

b. _____

c. _____

In what respect is exercise a poor way to lose weight? _____

_____

In what respect is exercise an excellent way to lose weight? _____

_____

_____

Define Food Exchange Systems: _____

_____

_____

What must a person do if he or she is to lose weight successfully and permanently?

a. _____

b. _____

20. What are the dietary goals suggested by the U. S. Senate Select Commission on Nutrition and Human Needs?

_____

_____

_____

_____

_____

_____

What percentage of protein, carbohydrates, and fats are recommended by this commission for the following:

a. protein? _____

b. carbohydrates? _____

c. fats? _____

PERSONAL SYNTHESIS

Knowing and accepting the realities of our physical self is one of the most important of our developmental tasks. Using your knowledge from Chapter 4, and your reflection in a full-length mirror, record your major physical attributes.

My major physical strengths are: _____

_____

_____

_____

_____

_____

My major physical weaknesses are: _____

_____

_____

_____

_____

Are you primarily lean, stout, or muscular? _____

_____

In what ways do your personality traits cluster around the expected traits of your body type?

_____

_____

_____

_____

_____

Have you ever been stigmatized because of your age, sex, race, or other attribute of your physical self?

_____

If you have been, recall the experience and your reactions to such discrimination:

_____

_____

_____

_____

_____

_____

_____

How important is personal attractiveness to you in selecting a date? _____

_____

_____

_____

How important is physical attractiveness to you in selecting a life's mate?

_____

_____

_____

Is there a contradiction between your mate/date value rating? _____

If the answer is yes, explain the contradiction: _____

_____

_____

_____

_____

_____

Do you employ situational and dispositional attribution to your own actions as
was described in Chapter 4?

_____

_____

Do you think this is necessary to maintain mental health? _____

_____

Or does it prevent one from attaining mental health? _____

_____

Does your current exercise program meet your physical goals? _____

_____

If not, what specific plan could you employ to achieve and maintain fitness?

_____

_____

_____

What are the chief blocks to acting on such a plan? _____

_____

_____

How do your current eating habits compare to the All American Diet? _____

_____

_____

What adjustments would you have to make to acheive the recommended daily percentages of protein, carbohydrates, and fats?

_____

_____

_____

SELF QUIZ

True or False

1. _____   Changing our energy consumption to regulate our body heat is one example of homeostasis.

2. _____   The most careful and extensive studies of body type and temperament were those done by Sheldon.

3. _____   Anxiety is more prevalent among the muscular and less prevalent among the lean and fat populations.

4. _____   People positively reinforce our behavior when we act as we are expected to act.

5. _____   People react to the elderly primarily in terms of the degree to which the elderly exhibit the changes in physical structure

and function that accompany the aging process.

6. _____ Concepts can be learned by direct or vicarious experiences. The body of theory relating to the "use of inferences and implied causality under conditions of minimal information" is known as psychosomatic theory.

7. _____ For most Americans, our jobs fail us when it comes to maintaining physical fitness.

8. _____ Your target heart rate for aerobic training should be approximately 30% of your maximum heart rate.

9. _____ Obesity for some people may be due to early feeding patterns that produced a permanent excess of fat cells.

10. _____ The only proven way to lose weight successfully and permanently is to adopt an eating plan that provides balanced nutrition at the appropriate level, and to stay with such a plan until your target weight has been reached.

Fill in the Blanks

11. Each species has a unique mor_____, and a bio-engineer can describe the limits of its performance.

12. Fast reactions, a quiet demeanor, and a love of privacy are characteristics of c_____.

13. Ilg and Ames advise new parents to accept the fact that their plump, pear-shaped infant e_____ will be sociable and easygoing.

14. Allport believes that our "_____" remains a lifelong anchor for our self-awareness.

15. A person introduced to a college class as a fellow student would appear to be _____ than the same person introduced to the class as a professor.

16. Attributing our praiseworthy acts to positive values and successful strategies is known as _____ determinism.

17. Three of the six goals of physical training stated by Van Huss are

_____, _____ and

_____.

18. Gently and slowly extending, holding, and turning each bodily joint is part of _____ training.

19. Obese people have _____ muscle proficiency than do

their thinner counterparts.

20. The Great American Diet contains quite a bit less _____
    and _____ than Americans now consume.

Answers and Question Numbers in REVIEW QUESTIONS section of chapter.

1. True (1, 2)

2. True (3)

3. False (9, 10)

4. True (12)

5. True (14, 15)

6. False (17)

7. True (21)

8. False (28, 29)

9. True (34, 35)

10. False (36, 37, 38)

11. morphogenotype (4, 5)

12. cerebrotonia (6, 7, 8)

13. endomorph (11)

14. "bodily me" (13)

15. taller (16)

16. dispositional (18, 19)

17. see chapter (23, 24)

18. flexibility (26, 27)

19. less (31, 32)

20. protein, fat (39, 40)

Chapter
FIVE

Sexual Self

CHAPTER TERMS AND CONCEPTS

The following terms and concepts are considered essential to an understanding of the material presented in Chapter 5, "Sexual Self."

1. gender
2. sexual illusions
3. male-female differences
4. sexual development (physical)
5. physique and sexuality
6. patterns of sexual response
7. phases of sexual response
8. sexual identification
9. sex role anxiety and hostility
10. gender and role disorders
11. rehearsal play
12. Victorian morality
13. learned competency
14. sexual dysfunctions
15. sexual re-education
16. coital positions
17. sexual variations
18. opportunity costs
19. contraception
20. developmental tasks

BEHAVIORAL OBJECTIVES

After reading and reflecting on the material presented in Chapter 5, "Sexual Self," you should be able to:

1. define human sexuality in terms of gender identification, roles, and preferences;

2. list several sex differences that are not the "illusions" of social conditioning;

3. describe the influence of sexual hormones on the development of our anatomy and physiology;

4. list the major advantages and disadvantages of current birth control practices and devices;

5. describe the <u>four phases of the sexual response</u> and the most common <u>sexual dysfunctions</u>;

6. Compare and contrast our <u>religious ideal</u> of sexual morality with selected <u>sexual variations</u>.

SEARCH FOR MEANING

Complete the following statements after locating the appropriate information as it appears in Chapter 4.

1. Define each of the following terms:

    a. Gender Role: _____

    _____

    b. Gender Identity: _____

    _____

    c. Gender Preference: _____

    _____

2. Relate <u>situational determinism</u> and <u>dispositional determinism</u> to the concept of the "illusion of sex differences."

    _____

    _____

    _____

    _____

3. List several non-illusionary differences that exist between average male and female behavior patterns:

    _____

    _____

    _____

    _____

    _____

4. Briefly describe the influence of sex hormones in the development of human internal and external sex organs.

_____

_____

_____

_____

_____

5. List ways in which our physical structure predisposes us to sexual activity:

_____

_____

_____

_____

a. How is the male sexual self manifested at birth? _____

_____

b. How is the female sexual self manifested at birth? _____

_____

c. What is the role of male penis and female breast size in effective sexual functioning?

_____

_____

_____

_____

6. In what ways are sound, touch, smell, and vision related to sexual behavior?

_____

_____

_____

_____

7. Briefly describe the four phases of human sexual response:

a. 1st phase: _____

_____

b. 2nd phase: _____

_____

c. 3rd phase: _____

_____

d. 4th phase: _____

_____

8. Sexual identification is largely a learned response. Explain gender
    identification, role, and preference in terms of:

    a. Freudian theory: _____

    _____

    _____

    b. Social learning theory: _____

    _____

    _____

    c. Cognitive theory: _____

    _____

    _____

9. Why does Lynn believe that males have a:

    a. stronger gender preference than do females? _____

    _____

    _____

    b. greater sex role anxiety? _____

    _____

    _____

    c. greater hostility towards the opposite sex? _____

_____

_____

10. Define the following:

a. paraphilia _____

_____

_____

b. transexualism _____

_____

_____

c. transvestism _____

_____

_____

d. bisexualism _____

_____

_____

11. What is the historical position of western religion on such matters as
pleasure, worldliness, and sexual expression?

_____

_____

_____

_____

12. In what way did the science of the Victorian Age influence our attitudes
towards sexual expression?

_____

_____

_____

_____

13. Give a brief example of <u>sexual</u> <u>rehearsal</u> during:

   a. infancy and childhood _____

   _____

   b. adolescence and young adulthood _____

   _____

   c. adulthood and middle age _____

   _____

   d. old age _____

   _____

14. Sexual dysfunctions are the result of genetics, injury, disease, and faulty learning. List the two major physical dysfunctions of:

   a. males _____

   _____

   b. females _____

   _____

15. In general terms, describe Masters' and Johnson's <u>educational</u> <u>approach</u> to the treatment of typical sexual dysfunctions:

   _____

   _____

   _____

   _____

   _____

   What four concepts do Masters and Johnson teach and reinforce concerning attitudes towards sex and sexual expression?

   a. _____

   b. _____

   c. _____

   d. _____

16. There appears to be no single, natural, and normal coital position. Each must be learned. List an advantage of each of the four basic positions:

    a. _____

    b. _____

    c. _____

    d. _____

17. Freud considered sexual activity to be instinctive. Select one example of a sexual variation that does <u>not</u> meet Freud's idea of "normal" sexual behavior, and explain in what way or ways it does not meet his criteria:

    _____

    _____

    _____

    _____

    _____

18. Define sexual opportunity costs: _____

    _____

    _____

    What costs, other than money costs, are associated with maintaining an active sex life during early adulthood?

    _____

    _____

    _____

19. Birth control practices are based on the realities of our sexual physiology. They often fail because of the realities of our psychology of sex. Select any three forms of birth control and list an advantage and disadvantage associated with each practice:

    a. _____

    _____

    b. _____

    _____

c. _____

_____

What variables, other than degree of effectiveness, do you consider important in the selection of a method of birth regulation?

_____

_____

_____

_____

20. According to <u>Cosmopolitan</u> magazine, what percentage of sexually active American women use absolutely no form of birth control? _____%

Why is an acceptance of our sexual self a necessary requirement for a satisfying and responsible life style?

_____

_____

_____

_____

_____

PERSONAL SYNTHESIS

Your sexual self forms a central component of your self-concept. Reflect upon the fact, theory, and tradition that you have reviewed in Chapter 5. Apply this information in answering the following questions concerning your sexuality:

1. What beliefs do you hold about basic behavioral and perceptual differences between the sexes?

_____

_____

_____

_____

2. What visual imagery is typically associated with your erotic fantasy?

_____

_____

_____

_____

3. What aspects of your gender identification and role cause you the most
   anxiety at present?

_____

_____

_____

4. In what ways are you hostile toward members of the opposite sex? _____

_____

_____

_____

In what ways are you compassionate towards them? _____

_____

_____

_____

5. Were your parents permissive in their tolerance of your early sexual
   rehearsal?

_____

In what ways have you been shaped by their level of tolerance? _____

_____

_____

_____

6. What attitudes, habits, and skills are you now learning, rehearsing, and
   incorporating into your sexual response patterns?

_____

_____

7. In what important ways are you now more accepting of the realities of your sexual identify?

_____

_____

_____

8. Finally, in what important ways are you pressing against illusionary sexual expectations that you feel are detrimental to your growth as a person?

_____

_____

_____

_____

_____

_____

SELF QUIZ

True or False

1. _____   Identity, preference, and role are components of our masculine/feminine gender.

2. _____   Kagen and Moss find that aggressive behavior is more intense and stable among female infants.

3. _____   The fetal brain requires a surplus of androgen to develop into a male brain.

4. _____   The uterus does not respond to sexual arousal; it is a reproductive, not sexual organ.

5. _____   Females are more anxious of their gender identification than are males.

6. _____   Sexual permissiveness during infancy and childhood appears to encourage the development of a strong, heterosexual identity and role.

7. _____   Between the ages of fifteen and nineteen, the percentage of Americans experiencing first intercourse increases steadily.

8. _____ Masters and Johnson employ radically different treatments for male and female sexual dysfunctions.

9. _____ Kinsey found more autoerotic, and less heterosexual or homo-sexual behavior among college-bound youngsters.

10. _____ At present, authorities are in agreement on the best method of birth control for everyone.

Fill in the Blanks

11. Maccoby and Jacklin find _____ non-illusionary differences between males and females.

12. During the first weeks following conception, the sex organs of males and females are _____.

13. List the four phases of the sexual response cycle: (1) _____

_____, (2) _____,

(3) _____, and (4) _____.

14. Men develop a consistent gender identity _____, and with _____ certainty than do females.

15. Erotic imagery, necessary for sexual arousal and performance, but other than that of an appropriate sexual partner is termed _____

_____.

16. Traditional Christian theology associated pl_____ and wo_____ with tolerance of sexual rehearsal, and helped shape our current beliefs about sex and morality.

17. The most common male sexual problem is _____ dysfunction.

18. The most common female sexual problem is _____ dysfunction.

19. According to Shah and Selnik, college _____ are not, in general, promiscuous.

20. At this time, the burden and responsibility for birth control falls heavily on _____.

Answers and Question Numbers in REVIEW QUESTIONS section of chapter.

1. True (1, 2, 3, 29)

2. False (5, 6, 8)

3. True (8, 9, 10, 11)

4. False (12, 14, 15)

5. False (27, 28)

6. True (37)

7. True (38, 39, 40)

8. False (45)

9. True (46, 47)

10. False (51, 52, 53, 54, 55)

11. few (4)

12. identical (7, 8)

13. Excitement, Plateau, Orgasm, Resolution (17, 18)

14. later, less (23, 24, 25, 26)

15. paraphilia (30, 31)

16. pleasure, worldliness (37)

17. erectile (42, 43, 44)

18. orgasmic (42, 43, 44)

19. women (48)

20. women (59)

Chapter
SIX

Cognitive Self

CHAPTER TERMS AND CONCEPTS

The following terms and concepts are considered essential to an understanding of the material presented in Chapter 6, "Cognitive Self."

1. cognition
2. cognitive control
3. cognitive formation
4. cognitive development
5. anticipatory schemes
6. psychological present
7. buffer delay
8. short term memory
9. long term memory
10. cognitive world

11. cognitive dissonance
12. cognition and emotion
13. affective dispositions
14. internal dialogue
15. Rational-Emotive Therapy
16. catastrophising
17. cognitive styles
18. rational thoughts
19. learned helplessness
20. learned resourcefulness

BEHAVIORAL OBJECTIVES

After reading and reflecting on the material presented in Chapter 6, "Cognitive Self," you should be able to:

1. define cognition and identify basic cognitive processes;

2. relate the limits of cognition to problems of adjustment;

3. describe cognitive styles and specific irrational beliefs that are associated with adjustment problems;

4. accept the notion that learned resourcefulness can be acquired through insight and cognitive conditioning.

SEARCH FOR MEANING

Complete the following statements after locating the appropriate information as it appears in Chapter 6.

1. Cognition is the process by which we derive meaning from experience.
    Cognition is defined as:

    _____

    _____

2. The constant flow of information to our nervous system must be controlled
    if we are not to be engulfed in a sea of sensations. Two avenues to
    cognitive control are:

    a. _____

        _____

    b. _____

        _____

3. Cognition is grounded in action. Our brain structure is partially con-
    trolled by genetics, and partially controlled by experience. Describe
    how a child, interacting with a series of balls, develops an abstract
    idea of the mental concept, ball:

    _____

    _____

    _____

    _____

    _____

4. Explain how our "ability to copy may be limited to the degree that our
    attention is free and can be directed to the events to be learned."

    _____

    _____

    _____

    _____

5. Compare and contrast the anticipatory schemes of an infant, a chess

amateur, and a chess master: _____

_____

_____

_____

_____

How are anticipatory schemes related to the perceptual cycle and to decisions of adjustment?

_____

_____

_____

6. Survival demands that we be able to hold some information in store while we process it. Otherwise, we could respond only to simple, one-dimensional problems. Define our "psychological present," or consciousness:

_____

_____

_____

7. How does our brain react when it receives more information than it can process at one time?

_____

_____

8. It is said that our short term memory allows us to be the master of our planet. Define short term memory:

_____

_____

a. How does this capacity help us make mental decisions? _____

_____

_____

b. How do the limits of short term memory hinder problem solving? _____

_____

_____

c. How can we delay the fading of information from memory? _____

_____

_____

9. Long term memory allows us to profit from experience. Define long term
    memory:

_____

_____

Is knowledge a recording or a reconstruction of past events? Explain
your answer:

_____

_____

_____

_____

10. We live in a world of objects. We also live in a world of ideas. Explain
    how these two ideas support the idea that our cognitive world is one of
    our own choosing and our own making.

    a. Perceptual schemata: _____

_____

_____

    b. Internal reconstruction of experience: _____

_____

_____

_____

c. How does our self-concept serve as an anchor for reality? _____

_____

_____

11. If we discover that our best friend admires our worst enemy, we are thrown off balance. Define cognitive dissonance:

_____

_____

_____

How do we maintain contact with reality while we distort reality in order to ensure psychological equilibrium?

_____

_____

_____

12. Explain the statement, "Emotion forms a common background for all of our knowledge."

_____

_____

_____

13. Our earliest cognitions are surrounded by intense emotion. Describe how early experience can affect our cognitive style, our affective disposition:

_____

_____

_____

14. Self-talk can guide and direct our feelings and actions. Define internal dialogue:

_____

_____

_____

How can healthy self-talk help us in stressful situations?

a. _____

b. _____

Luria describes a three-stage process by which one gains silent, verbal control of motor acts. These three steps are:

a. _____

b. _____

c. _____

15. List at least four common <u>irrational beliefs</u> that Albert Ellis thinks lead to negative emotions and poor behavior:

a. _____

b. _____

c. _____

d. _____

16. Define:

a. <u>catastrophising</u>: _____

_____

b. <u>musterbating</u>: _____

_____

In what ways may catastrophising and musterbating combine to produce or increase problems of adjustment?

_____

_____

_____

17. Patterns of thinking, as well as specific thoughts, can be the source of adjustment problems. Define <u>cognitive styles</u>:

_____

_____

_____

Give two examples of how Beck trains his clients to challenge and change their dysfunctional thought patterns:

a. _____

_____

b. _____

_____

18. List three <u>rational</u> <u>thoughts</u> that cognitive-behavioral therapists believe will reduce the pressure to be perfect and to expect perfection from others:

a. _____

b. _____

c. _____

19. Define and give an example of <u>learned</u> <u>helplessness</u>: _____

_____

_____

Relate learned helplessness to feelings of depression: _____

_____

_____

20. Cognitive style and content can be modified and applied to the solution of complex adjustment problems. List the four areas in which the Goldfrieds train their clients to make positive statements and so master <u>learned</u> <u>resourcefulness</u>.

a. _____

_____

b. _____

_____

c. _____

_____

d. _____

_____

PERSONAL SYNTHESIS

     Nothing could possibly be as unique and personal as our own private
thoughts and style of thinking. Reflect a moment on the structure of your
mind, the capacities and limits of your intellect, and the specific mental
baggage that you bring to life's encounters.

     Using as many of the terms and concepts from Chapter 6 as you can, assess
the mental assets and liabilities that you possess at this moment. Be sure to
include both any mental resources that you can count on, and any rigid ideas
or patterns of thinking that seem to be holding you back.

_____

_____

_____

_____

_____

_____

_____

_____

_____

_____

_____

_____

_____

_____

_____

_____

_____

_____

SELF QUIZ

True or False

1. _____ Cognition is the act of acquiring, organizing, and using knowledge.

2. _____ When we assimilate new information, we change our existing schema to fit the new input.

3. _____ For about three-quarters of a second, we are able to retain unprocessed information as direct representations of past experiences.

4. _____ Our cognitive world is largely of our own choosing (perceptual schemata) and of our own making (internal reconstruction).

5. _____ Individuals are unable to deny, distort, or reject reality so as to reduce cognitive dissonance.

6. _____ Our knowledge remains separate from our emotions.

7. _____ A child gains verbal control of voluntary motor acts in part by imitating the speech of significant others.

8. _____ Viewing every non-perfect event as a personal calamity is termed "catastrophising."

9. _____ People who view cognitions as behavior that can be modified are said to suffer from learned helplessness.

10. _____ After successful therapy, Beck's clients are more capable of viewing negative events as tragic and catastrophic rather than merely disappointing and unfortunate.

Fill in the Blanks

11. Two avenues to cognitive control are (a) the ability to _____ relevant clues, and (b) a meaningful search for connections.

12. According to Piaget, _____ is the most important element in cognition.

13. A richness of an_____ sc_____, rather than higher intelligence, separates the chess master from the amateur.

14. The sensory inputs that we receive during any _____ second period are perceived as one impression.

15. After attending to a bit of information, we can hold it in memory for approximately _____ seconds.

16. Long term memory, or knowledge, is thought to be an int _____
rec _____ of past events.

17. If our first experiences were largely good ones, we learn positive emotional predispositions that form a basic portion of our c _____
s _____.

18. The basic premise of cognitive therapists is that emotional suffering and inappropriate behavior are due to i _____ b _____.

19. Beck's clinical population makes _____ inferences, _____ the importance of single events, and _____ events as being all good or all bad.

20. Using process statements to guide a problem solving series of steps is termed l _____ r _____
by the Goldfrieds.

Answers and Question Numbers in REVIEW QUESTIONS section of chapter.

1. True (9)   11. focus on (4)

2. False (16)   12. action (11)

3. True (29)   13. anticipatory schemes (20, 23)

4. True (34)   14. 1/10 second (28)

5. False (37)   15. 10 seconds (30)

6. False (38)   16. internal reconstruction (33)

7. True (46)   17. cognitive style (39)

8. True (50)   18. irrational beliefs (50)

9. False (53)   19. faulty, overgeneralize, over-
                                       simplify (51)

10. False (52)   20. learned resourcefulness (53)

Chapter
SEVEN

Emotional Self

CHAPTER TERMS AND CONCEPTS

The following terms and concepts are considered essential to an understanding of the material presented in Chapter 7, "Emotional Self."

1. emotion
2. value of emotions
3. the social smile
4. negative expression
5. the James/Lange Theory
6. Autonomic Nervous System
7. the Cannon/Bard Theory
8. Limbic System
9. Cognitive Theory
10. Pro- and Anti-social emotions

11. appropriateness
12. intensity
13. expression
14. trust and openness
15. depression
16. Cognition-behavioral View
17. learned helplessness
18. love
19. love as an attitude
20. acceptance and empathy

BEHAVIORAL OBJECTIVES

After reading and reflecting on the material presented in Chapter 7, "Emotional Self," you should be able to:

1. list several current definitions of emotion;

2. describe the function of emotions in species survival;

3. be aware of the human need for freedom to express a wide range of emotional experiences;

4. differentiate among theories of emotion such as the James/Lange and Cannon/Bard Theories;

5. list examples of failures in emotional intensity, expression, and appropriateness;

6. compare and contrast the emotions of love and depression.

SEARCH FOR MEANING

Complete the following statements after locating the appropriate information as it appears in Chapter 7.

1. What is <u>emotion</u>? _____

_____

_____

_____

_____

What is always a component of any aroused state? _____

_____

_____

2. Charles Darwin wrote <u>The Expression of the Emotions in Man and Animals</u>.

    a. List some evidence to support the contention that emotional expression is innate:

    _____

    _____

    _____

    _____

    b. Give an example of the <u>survival</u> value of emotion: _____

    _____

    _____

    c. Why does the <u>signal</u> value of an emotion function to reduce combat within a species?

    _____

    _____

3. The <u>first</u> <u>smile</u> in humans is in response to: _____

What is the purpose of the infant's cry, according to John Bowlby?

_____

_____

4. How does the emotional development of the infant differ from that of the two and one-half year old child?

_____

_____

_____

a. What are the effects of tolerating a relatively large amount of negative emotional expression by the young child?

_____

_____

_____

b. What are the effects of harsh and frequent spankings, according to Gilmartin?

_____

_____

5. Describe the James/Lange Theory of Emotion: _____

_____

_____

_____

_____

Briefly define:

a. The Central Nervous System: _____

_____

b. The Peripheral Nervous System: _____

_____

6. **Differentiate** between the Sympathetic and the Parasympathetic Nervous Systems:

    _____

    _____

    _____

    _____

7. List three criticisms of the James/Lange Theory, as presented by Cannon and Bard:

    a. _____

    b. _____

    c. _____

    Describe the path of emotional neural impulses as outlined by Cannon and Bard:

    _____

    _____

    _____

    _____

8. Emotions may be controlled by a <u>complex circuit</u> in our brains. Briefly identify the <u>Limbic System</u> and the <u>Reticular Formation</u> as emotional coding mechanisms:

    _____

    _____

    _____

    _____

9. How did Schachter and Singer give experimental support to their Cognitive Theory of Emotion?

    _____

    _____

    _____

    _____

Give an example of a typical _internal_ _dialogue_ that might be encountered during an emotionally intense bout with _anger_:

_____

_____

_____

_____

10. Differentiate between pro-social and anti-social emotions: _____

_____

_____

List three pro-social emotions:

a. _____

b. _____

c. _____

List three anti-social emotions:

a. _____

b. _____

c. _____

11. Define emotional appropriateness: _____

_____

_____

Why do others judge the _appropriateness_ of your emotional expression?

_____

_____

_____

12. Under what circumstances does emotional _intensity_ become an emotional problem of adjustment?

_____

_____

a. What is sensory deprivation? _____

_____

How is this related to emotions and mind control? _____

_____

_____

c. State the Yerkes/Dodson Law: _____

_____

d. How is the Type A Personality associated with emotional intensity and physiological disorder?

_____

_____

13. What percentage of a complete message is conveyed by:

a. what we say? _____

b. how we say it? _____

c. our facial expression while saying it? _____

List additional ways in which we communicate emotional information:

_____

_____

_____

14. What is Fritz Perls' position on emotional expression and mental health?

_____

_____

_____

Why do children learn to mistrust their own emotions and to restrict their emotional expression?

_____

_____

_____

15. Define <u>depression</u> according to:

    a. the psychotherapeutic viewpoint _____

        _____

        _____

    b. the behaviorist viewpoint _____

        _____

        _____

    c. the psychophysiological viewpoint _____

        _____

        _____

16. What three important <u>irrational</u> thoughts are typically held by depressed patients, according to Aaron Beck?

    a. _____

    b. _____

    c. _____

17. Define <u>learned helplessness</u>: _____

_____

_____

_____

Give examples of ways in which you could help your children to resist learning learned helplessness:

_____

_____

_____

18. What is love, according to Libbowitz and Klien? _____

_____

_____

_____

List three useful properties of the emotion "love":

a. _____

b. _____

c. _____

List three potentially dangerous properties of the emotion "love":

a. _____

b. _____

c. _____

19. Zick Rubin sees love as an attitude. What three dimensions does this attitude contain?

a. _____

b. _____

c. _____

What role does passion play in this mental conception of love? _____

_____

_____

20. What are the cornerstones of a helping relationship, according to Carl Rogers?

_____

_____

_____

Why is each of these two emotions essential to forming an intimate bond with another human being?

_____

_____

_____

_____

PERSONAL SYNTHESIS

    We feel, and feeling transforms our daily existence into our sense of being alive. Reflect a moment on a period of your life when you felt fatigued and depressed. In what important ways has a study of this chapter helped you to understand your physical and emotional self during this trying period? What have you learned that might prevent, reduce, or shorten any future periods of depression?

_____

_____

_____

_____

_____

_____

_____

_____

_____

_____

_____

_____

_____

_____

_____

_____

_____

_____

_____

_____

In what important ways can you apply your knowledge of emotion to increase the amount of pro-social emotions being felt and expressed within your family and friendship circles?

_____

_____

_____

_____

_____

_____

_____

_____

_____

_____

_____

_____

_____

_____

_____

_____

_____

_____

_____

_____

_____

SELF QUIZ

<u>True</u> or <u>False</u>

1. _____ We cannot experience an emotion without changes taking place in our nervous system, internal organs, and glands.

2. _____ The initial sign of infant love is the appearance of a smile.

3. _____ William James holds that, "We do not run because we are afraid, but rather that we are afraid because we run."

4. _____ The Limbic System of our brain is a complex structure that underlies our feelings and influences our emotional behavior, according to Papez.

5. _____ Pro-social emotions tend to inhibit interpersonal relations.

6. _____ The appropriateness of an emotion is determined by a rational cognitive appraisal of the ongoing situation.

7. _____ The ability to correctly interpret the emotions contained in a facial expression increases with age.

8. _____ To learn NOT to show feelings may lessen one's capacity to have feelings.

9. _____ Behavior similar to human depresson cannot now be produced in laboratory animals.

10. _____ Carl Rogers sees empathy and acceptance as the cornerstones of a loving (helping) relationship.

<u>Fill</u> <u>in</u> <u>the</u> <u>Blanks</u>

11. In aggressive animals, the emotional expression of courtship behavior such as affection and passion, have both s_____ and signal value.

12. Children who are _____ often and harshly for expressing negative emotions are found to be quieter, less articulate, and more sullen than less harshly treated children.

13. Cannon and Bard believe that incoming neural impulses reach our <u>cortex</u> and block the normal <u>in</u>_____ of the hypothalamus.

14. The Autonomic Nervous System is itself divided into the s_____ and the p_____ nervous systems.

15. The Cognitive Theory of Emotion states that we engage in a c_____ a_____ of the psychological situation prior to labeling our emotions and giving them expression.

16. The dimension that differentiates between apprehension, fear, and terror is _____.

17. Depression is complicated by the fact that it contains two additional negative emotions, guilt and _____.

18. Depressives blame _____ for their problems, and see life as a continuous encounter with tragic misfortunes and failures.

19. Zick Rubin looks at love as an attitude containing the dimensions of attachment, _____, and intimacy.

20. To Elaine Walster, romantic love is a state of p_____
    a_____ that is defined as love.

Answers and Question Numbers in REVIEW QUESTIONS section of chapter.

1. True (1)	11. survival (2)
2. False (3)	12. spanked (punished) (10, 12)
3. True (13, 14, 15)	13. inhibition (16)
4. True (17, 18, 19)	14. sympathetic, parasympathetic (13)
5. False (23)	15. cognitive appraisal (21, 22, 23)
6. False (21, 24)	16. intensity (26, 31)
7. True (26, 28)	17. anger (31, 35)
8. True (30)	18. themselves (36)
9. False (35)	19. caring (38)
10. True (45)	20. physiological arousal (39)

PART THREE ADJUSTMENT AND GROWTH

Chapter

EIGHT

Stress

CHAPTER TERMS AND CONCEPTS

The following terms and concepts are considered essential to an understanding of the material presented in Chapter 8, "Stress."

1. stress
2. stressor
3. flight/fight response
4. restorative response
5. diseases of adaptation
6. General Adaptation Syndrome
7. emotional death
8. autoimmune system
9. anxiety
10. mental illness and stress
11. job-related stress
12. optimum stress levels
13. stress and behavioral change
14. Rahe's transformations
15. direct coping
16. defensive coping
17. repressors
18. sensitizers
19. self-modulation
20. biofeedback

BEHAVIORAL OBJECTIVES

After reading and reflecting on the material presented in Chapter 8, "Stress," you should be able to:

1. define stress and identify psychological and physical stressors;

2. describe the flight/fight response to stress;

3. identify physical and mental illnesses associated with prolonged, unresolved stress;

4. list specific forms of job-related stress for both professional and non-professional careers;

5. list and define indirect coping mechanisms such as repression and substance abuse;

6. describe the restorative response and methods of cultivating a state of low arousal.

SEARCH FOR MEANING

Complete the following statements after locating the appropriate information as it appears in Chapter 8.

1. Define <u>stress</u>: _____

_____

_____

2. The human is capable of responding stressfully to a wide range of stimuli. List the four categories of stressors, and give an example of each:

   a. _____

   b. _____

   c. _____

   d. _____

3. Describe the Flight/Fight Response:

   a. Under ancient conditions _____

   _____

   _____

   b. Under modern conditions _____

   _____

   _____

4. Define the <u>restorative response</u>: _____

_____

_____

In what forms does stress remain in us when we cannot completely discharge the energy mobilized by stress?

_____

_____

_____

_____

5. Physical illness that is produced or augmented by unresolved stress is
    termed by Hans Selye to be:

    _____

    a. What are psychosomatic disorders? _____

        _____

        _____

    b. Define the G. A. S.: _____

        _____

        _____

6. List the three stages of the G. A. S.:

    a. _____

    b. _____

    c. _____

7. What three factors appear to be necessary if a healthy person is to be in
    danger of suffering emotional death?

    a. _____

    b. _____

    c. _____

8. Identify NCKA and describe the relationship of NCKA to:

    a. stress levels _____

        _____

        _____

    b. ability to cope with stress _____

        _____

9. Describe the roots of anxiety as seen by:

    a. Garre _____

b. Horney _____

c. Existential Thought _____

10. What is the relationship between perceived stress levels and the presence of mental problems as reported by Vinokur and Selzer?

_____

_____

11. What relationship was found by Glass and Singer to hold true between noise levels and stress?

_____

_____

_____

Under what conditions is a longer ride to work less stressful than a shorter one?

_____

_____

List three of the most stressful jobs as reported by Dr. Smith:

a. _____

b. _____

c. _____

List three of the least stressful jobs as reported by Dr. Smith:

a. _____

b. _____

c. _____

12. List four _positive_ effects of being under moderate stress, as seen by Hebb:

a. _____

b. _____

c. _____

d. _____

Describe several forms of <u>eustress</u> considered to be necessary for our
well-being and self-esteem:

_____

_____

_____

_____

13. Albert Bandura believes that there are four sources of information needed
for the successful change of human behavior. All involve stress. What
are these sources?

a. _____

_____

b. _____

_____

c. _____

_____

d. _____

_____

14. Richard Rahe suggests that there are six <u>transformations</u> that a stress
response must go through before it is officially labeled a medical illness.
What are they?

a. _____

b. _____

c. _____

d. _____

e. _____

f. _____

15. Define <u>direct coping</u>: _____

_____

_____

Give two examples of direct coping actions that might be harmful to yourself, or to others:

a. _____

b. _____

16. Why does Gary Schwartz define indirect coping actions as "disregulators?"

_____

_____

_____

Why do we use defensive coping? _____

_____

_____

17. Describe a <u>repressor</u>: _____

_____

Select three defense mechanisms used by repressors, and describe them:

a. _____

b. _____

c. _____

18. Describe a <u>sensitizer</u>: _____

_____

Select any three defense mechanisms used by sensitizers and describe them:

a. _____

b. _____

c. _____

19. Why is the term "modulation" more suitable than regulation or control in describing attempts to make our stress responses work for us?

_____

_____

20. Define <u>biofeedback</u>: _____

_____

_____

What is <u>passive</u> <u>attention</u>, and how is it related to success in relaxation training?

_____

_____

_____

_____

PERSONAL SYNTHESIS

Stress will always be with us. What bothers us, and how we respond to these situations, are to a large extent under our voluntary control. Using the following terms, or ideas, complete the following chart of (1) what situations now cause you repeated stress, (2) how you now respond to that stress, and (3) possible ways in which you think you could modulate your stress responses.

STRESS RESPONSE SYNTHESIS

_____

(material from next page)

_____

RESPONSES	STRESSFUL SITUATIONS					
Pattern of Responding to Stress	School – Job		Home – Recreation		Social – Sexual	
	Describe Situation:		Describe Situation:		Describe Situation:	
	At Present	Possible Alternative	At Present	Possible Alternative	At Present	Possible Alternative
Physiological heart beat, relaxation, etc. How my body responds.						
Psychological defense mechanism, coping, strategies, etc. How my mind responds.						
Emotional anger, fear, humor, etc. How I feel when stressed.						
Cognitive "This is a disaster," or "I can handle this," etc., How I talk to myself.						
Behavioral Running, cursing, smoking, laughing, etc. What I do.						

SELF QUIZ

<u>True</u> or <u>False</u>

1. _____ Stress is a nonspecific response to any demand placed upon us.

2. _____ The Flight/Fight Response conserves energy to allow us to confront an enemy or to flee.

3. _____ The general, positive effects on our bodies from prolonged stress are termed diseases of adaptation.

4. _____ Emotional Death can be the result of experiencing profound excitement, a sense of loss of control, and a lack of social supports.

5. _____ Lymphocytes form a minor part of our autoimmune system.

6. _____ Higher frequencies of perceived stress are reported by persons diagnosed as suffering from a wide range of mental disorders, from paranoia through depression.

7. _____ Receiving eustress associated with recognition and responsibility is beneficial in reducing anxiety and building self-esteem.

8. _____ Indirect coping is acting so as to alter the environment that caused the stress we experience.

9. _____ Direct coping is less complex, more accessible, and promises quicker results than does indirect coping.

10. _____ An awareness of mind/body unity, and a renewed belief in preventative medicine has opened up novel approaches to the reduction of stress-related illnesses.

<u>Fill</u> <u>in</u> <u>the</u> <u>Blanks</u>

11. A sudden loud noise is an example of an _____ physical stressor.

12. The restorative response is characterized by _____ oxygen consumption, and _____ brain activity.

13. The three stages of the General Adaptation Syndrome are:

    (1) _____, (2) _____, and

    (3) _____.

14. "_____" anxiety is a constant facet of one's
    personality, while "_____" anxiety is a response
    to a specific stressor.

15. College graduates with a high need to achieve are often torn between being

    (1) _____ and being (2) _____.

16. List two of the four sources of information that Albert Bandura says are
    needed to bring about behavior change: (1) _____
    and (2) _____.

17. List three of the six transformations that Richard Rahe says a stress-
    related disorder must pass through before it is medically recognized as
    an illness: (1) _____, (2) _____,
    and (3) _____.

18. Three defense mechanisms used by repressors in indirect coping include:

    (1) _____, (2) _____ and (3) _____.

19. The major defense mechanisms employed by sensitizers include: (1) _____

    _____, (2) _____ and (3) _____.

20. List three stress-related disorders that have been relieved through the
    process of biofeedback training: (1) _____,

    (2) _____, and (3) _____.

Answers and Question Numbers in REVIEW QUESTIONS section of chapter.

1. True (4)

2. False (3)

3. False (9)

4. True (16)

5. False (18)

6. True (22)

7. True (30)

8. False (37)

9. False (38)

10. True (54)

11. unlearned (2)

12. lower, lower (7, 55)

13. Alarm, Resistance, Exhaustion (10)

14. Trait, State (21, 46)

15. well liked, aggressive (23, 25)

16. performance accomplishments, sensitized to physiological state, vicarious experiences, persuasion (34)

17. cognitive appraisal, ego-defense mechanisms, alarm and resistance, direct coping, exhaustion, diagnoses (36)

18. repression, denial, reaction-formation, displacement, sublimation, rationalization, regression (38, 40)

19. emotional insulation, physical isolation, intellectualization, projection, compensation, fantasizing, rationalization, conversion (45)

20. anxiety symptoms, headaches, bruxism, insomnia, menstrual cramps, asthma, high blood pressure, hyperhydrosis, pain, sexual dysfunction, social skills (53)

Chapter
NINE

Adjustment

CHAPTER TERMS AND CONCEPTS

The following terms and concepts are considered essential to an understanding of the material presented in Chapter 9, "Adjustment."

1. adjustment
2. neo-Freudians
3. existentialists
4. adjustment and values
5. compromise
6. growth
7. autonomy
8. adjustment strategies
9. dimensions of adjustment
10. planning

11. adjustment and self-esteem
12. adjustment and time
13. maladjustment
14. neurotic disorders
15. phobic disorders
16. obsessive compulsive disorder
17. personality disorders
18. psychotic disorders
19. schizophrenic disorders
20. paranoid disorders

BEHAVIORAL OBJECTIVES

After reading and reflecting on the material presented in Chapter 9,
"Adjustment," you should be able to:

1. discuss the relationship between a conception of good adjustment and
    social and cultural values;

2. list several factors that may be used to judge either the adequacy of any
    given individual response, or the adequacy of any given adjustment strategy;

3. discuss the ways in which human adjustment is significantly different from
    that of other animals;

4. define maladjustment and identify three major categories of maladjustment;

5. give examples of each of these three major categories of maladjustment.

SEARCH FOR MEANING

Complete the following statements after locating the appropriate information as it appears in Chapter 9.

1. Define good <u>adjustment</u> from each of the following viewpoints:

a. Fruedians _____

    _____

    _____

b. behaviorists _____

    _____

    _____

c. humanists _____

    _____

    _____

2. How have the <u>neo-Freudians</u> modified Freud's view of adjustment? _____

    _____

    How does Erik Erikson define good adjustment? _____

    _____

    _____

    _____

3. What is the <u>existentialist</u> definition of good adjustment? _____

    _____

    _____

    _____

4. List five <u>values</u> that Americans have traditionally used as barometers of good adjustment:

a. _____

b. _____

c. _____

d. _____

e. _____

Discuss the relationship between a conception of good adjustment and social and cultural values.

_____

_____

_____

_____

_____

_____

_____

_____

5. Why is <u>compromise</u> essential in order to survive? _____

_____

_____

_____

_____

_____

_____

_____

6. What is <u>growth</u>? _____

_____

_____

Give examples of each of the following types of growth:

a. physical _____

_____

b. psychological _____

_____

c. social _____

_____

7. What is <u>autonomy</u>? _____

_____

How may an increase in autonomy be considered a manifestation of growth?

_____

_____

_____

_____

8. What is an adjustment strategy? _____

_____

_____

What three criteria may be used to judge the adequacy of any given adjustment strategy?

a. _____

_____

b. _____

_____

c. _____

_____

9. Discuss three significant ways that human adjustment is different from
that of other animals:

a. _____

_____

_____

_____

_____

b. _____

_____

_____

_____

_____

c. _____

_____

_____

_____

_____

How are human adjustment strategies different from those of other animals?

_____

_____

_____

_____

_____

_____

_____

_____

_____

_____

_____

_____

_____

_____

_____

_____

_____

_____

_____

_____

10. Why is <u>planning</u> such an important factor in human adjustment? _____

_____

_____

_____

_____

_____

_____

11. Why is the maintenance of <u>self-esteem</u> such an important factor in human adjustment?

_____

_____

_____

_____

_____

_____

_____

12. Explain the <u>duration</u> <u>dimension</u> of the expanded time factor in a human's strategy for maintaining autonomy or freedom of movement.

_____

_____

_____

_____

_____

_____

13. What is <u>maladjustment</u>? _____

_____

_____

Name three major categories of maladjustment.

a. _____

b. _____

c. _____

14. What are <u>neurotic</u> <u>disorders</u>? _____

_____

_____

_____

15. What are <u>phobic</u> disorders? _____

_____

_____

Give two examples of phobic disorders:

a. _____

b. _____

16. What is <u>obsessive</u> <u>compulsive</u> <u>disorder</u>? _____

_____

_____

Give an example of an obsession: _____

_____

_____

_____

Give an example of a compulsion: _____

_____

_____

_____

17. What are <u>personality</u> <u>disorders</u>? _____

_____

_____

_____

_____

Give two examples of personality disorders:

a. _____

b. _____

18. What are <u>psychotic</u> <u>disorders</u>? _____

_____

_____

List four common characteristics of psychotic disorders:

a. _____

b. _____

c. _____

d. _____

19. What are some of the common characteristics of <u>schizophrenic disorders</u>?

_____

_____

_____

_____

_____

20. What are some of the common characteristics of <u>paranoid disorders</u>?

_____

_____

_____

_____

_____

PERSONAL SYNTHESIS

Reflect for a few minutes on your own life circumstances during the past year. Think about the relationships and events in your personal life, your college experience, and your work life.

Now, using as many of the terms and concepts from Chapter 9 as you can, identify some of the adjustment strategies you have used and judge them according to the three criteria presented in your textbook.

_____

_____

_____

_____

_____

_____

_____

_____

_____

SELF QUIZ

True or False

1. _____ All scholars agree that good <u>adjustment</u> is the individual's effective use of defense mechanisms to satisfy the demands of both the id and the superego simultaneously.

2. _____ The <u>neo-Freudians</u> emphasize ego functioning and the social nature of human beings.

3. _____ The <u>existentialists</u> emphasize responsibility for one's own behavior.

4. _____ It is impossible to evaluate good adjustment without making value judgments.

5. _____ <u>Compromise</u> is never a useful adjustment strategy.

6. _____ A <u>growing</u> organism is constantly taking materials from outside itself and transforming them into parts of its own.

7. _____ Living organisms are always governed completely by forces outside of themselves.

8. _____ <u>Strategies of adjustment</u> are fixed and never imply choice.

9. _____ Humans treat time, language, and morality in a significantly different fashion from other animals.

10. _____ <u>Planning</u> is never a significant factor in human adjustment.

Fill in the Blanks

11. An important psychological factor in human adjustment is the level of
s_____.

12. Any human strategy for maintaining autonomy or freedom of movement is different from that of other animals in two important ways: it has powerful psychological and social factors, and it has an e_____
t_____ f_____.

13. M_____ is the individual's relative failure to meet adequately the psychological demands of either himself or herself, the group, or the situation.

14. Some n_____ d_____ involve a disturbance of mood; others are related to anxiety; still others are associated with a sudden, temporary change in consciousness, identity, or motor behavior.

15. Intense and unrealistic fears are maladjustments referred to as
    p_____ d_____.

16. A person who repeatedly has a senseless or repugnant thought coming into
    his or her mind is suffering from an o_____.

17. A person who seems to lack a conscience and a concern for other people
    has a_____ p_____
    d_____.

18. Inappropriateness of emotional response, personality disorganization,
    hallucinations, and delusions are characteristics common to p_____
    d_____.

19. Maladjustments in which the person suffers a severe split between cog-
    nition and emotion are called s_____
    d_____.

20. The person suffering from a p_____ d_____
    is highly suspicious of other people and often misinterprets their actions,
    remarks, or gestures as intentional "put downs" designed to slight him or
    her in some way.

Answers and Question Numbers in REVIEW QUESTIONS section of chapter.

1. False (1)   11. self-esteem (15)

2. True (2)   12. expanded time factor (16)

3. True (4)   13. Maladjustment (18)

4. True (5)   14. neurotic disorders (19)

5. False (7)   15. phobic disorders (20)

6. True (8)   16. obsession (20)

7. False (8)   17. antisocial personality disorder (21)

8. False (9)   18. psychotic disorders (22)

9. True (11)   19. schizophrenic disorders (23)

10. False (13)   20. paranoid disorder (23)

Chapter
TEN

Psychotherapy

CHAPTER TERMS AND CONCEPTS

The following terms and concepts are considered essential to an understanding of the material presented in Chapter 10, "Psychotherapy."

1. psychotherapy
2. the need for therapy
3. types of therapists
4. psychoanalysis
5. neo-Freudian analysis
6. analytical psychology
7. existential approach
8. Rogerian therapy
9. Gestalt therapy
10. biofunctional therapy
11. primal therapy
12. group therapy
13. encounter groups
14. est
15. transactional analysis
16. somatic therapy
17. behavior therapy
18. cognitive therapy
19. choosing a therapy
20. risks of therapy

BEHAVIORAL OBJECTIVES

After reading and reflecting on the material presented in Chapter 10, "Psychotherapy," you should be able to:

1. define psychotherapy and identify at least three different ways of classifying therapies;

2. identify several different types of psychotherapists;

3. compare and contrast at least ten different therapies;

4. discuss several important factors involved in selecting both a therapist and a therapy.

SEARCH FOR MEANING

Complete the following statements after locating the appropriate information as it appears in Chapter 10.

1. What is <u>psychotherapy</u>? _____

_____

_____

2. People begin to sense that they may <u>need</u> some kind of help when they realize that things are not going well, but they do not know what to do to improve the situation. Examples might include:

a. _____

b. _____

c. _____

d. _____

3. Identify each of the following <u>types of therapists</u>:

a. psychiatrists _____

_____

_____

_____

_____

_____

b. psychologists _____

_____

_____

_____

_____

c. psychiatric social workers _____

_____

_____

_____

_____

_____

d. psychoanalysts _____

_____

_____

_____

e. sex therapists _____

_____

_____

f. psychiatric nurses _____

_____

_____

g. pastoral counselors _____

_____

_____

4. The first psychotherapy to have wide-ranging impact was Sigmund Freud's
    psychoanalysis. Below are listed four important aspects of psychoanalysis.
    Define and discuss the significance of each.

    a. free association _____

    _____

    _____

    _____

    _____

    _____

    _____

_____

_____

b. resistances _____

_____

_____

_____

_____

_____

_____

_____

c. transference _____

_____

_____

_____

_____

_____

_____

_____

_____

d. dream analysis _____

_____

_____

_____

_____

_____

5. Discuss the major differences between <u>neo-Freudian analysis</u> and <u>psycho-analysis</u>:

_____

_____

_____

_____

_____

_____

_____

_____

_____

_____

6. C. G. Jung's school of psychological thought is called <u>analytical psychology</u>. Define each of the following terms associated with analytical psychology:

a. collective unconscious _____

_____

_____

b. archetypes _____

_____

_____

c. anima _____

_____

d. animus _____

_____

e. shadow _____

_____

How does dream analysis in analytical psychology differ from dream analysis in psychoanalysis?

_____

_____

_____

_____

_____

_____

7. Explain the procedure that would be used by a therapist using the
    existential approach:

_____

_____

_____

_____

_____

_____

8. Discuss the basic technique of Rogerian therapy. Provide examples when-
    ever appropriate.

_____

_____

_____

_____

_____

_____

9. Why is awareness such an important factor in Gestalt therapy? Explain
    your answer.

_____

_____

_____

_____

_____

_____

_____

_____

10. How does <u>biofunctional therapy</u> differ from the analytic therapies?
    Explain.

    _____

    _____

    _____

    _____

    _____

    _____

    _____

11. The goal of <u>primal therapy</u> is to transform the patient's state of feeling.
    Why? Explain your answer.

    _____

    _____

    _____

    _____

    _____

12. List two of the advantages of <u>traditional group therapy</u> over individual
    psychoanalysis:

    a. _____

       _____

    b. _____

       _____

13. What is the primary focus of an <u>encounter group</u>? How might this help a
    person achieve better adjustment?

_____

_____

_____

_____

_____

14. What is the stated purpose of est? _____

_____

What are the three major components of the est training?

a. _____

b. _____

c. _____

15. Transactional analysis holds that a person's behavior at any given time is dominated by one of three ego states. Name and identify them:

a. _____

_____

b. _____

_____

c. _____

_____

16. Name and identify three different types of somatic therapy:

a. _____

_____

_____

b. _____

_____

_____

c. _____

_____

_____

17. Two techniques often used in <u>behavior therapy</u> are systematic desensitization and progressive relaxation. Explain each:

a. systematic desensitization _____

_____

_____

_____

_____

_____

b. progressive relaxation _____

_____

_____

_____

_____

_____

18. What is the fundamental notion upon which <u>cognitive therapy</u> is based?

_____

_____

_____

What two techniques do cognitive therapists invariably use?

a. _____

_____

b. _____

_____

19. Explain the following statement: "Some therapies may be better suited
than others to deal with certain problems." Provide examples whenever

appropriate. _____

_____

_____

_____

_____

_____

_____

_____

_____

20. Discuss some of the risks of successful therapy: _____

_____

_____

_____

_____

_____

_____

_____

_____

PERSONAL SYNTHESIS

Reflect for a few minutes on your own personality and locate a few areas in which you would like to improve your adjustment.

Now, using as many of the terms and concepts from Chapter 10 as you can, take yourself mentally through the process of selecting a therapy and a therapist to help you. Describe the therapy and the therapist, and tell why each is well suited to help you.

_____

_____

_____

SELF QUIZ

<u>True</u> or <u>False</u>

1. _____   <u>Psychotherapy</u> involves the use of psychological techniques to
help a person achieve better adjustment.

2. _____   People begin to sense that they may need help when they realize that things are not going well, but that the situation is
completely under control.

3. _____   Psychiatrists are the only therapists who can legally pre-
scribe drugs.

4. _____   <u>Psychoanalysis</u> involves two steps: strengthening the weakened
ego by extending its self-knowledge and breaking down
resistances.

5. _____   Neo-Freudian analysis emphasizes the drive toward self-
realization.

6. _____   <u>Analytical psychology</u> holds that in addition to the Freudian
"personal unconscious," there is a "personal conscious" that
reflects the cosmic order.

7. _____   According to the <u>existential approach</u>, it is through our own
choices that we construct an orderly and meaningful life for
ourselves.

8. _____   The basic technique of <u>Rogerian therapy</u> is for the therapist
to provide the client with unconditional positive regard.

9. _____   In <u>Gestalt therapy</u> the therapist's job is to get the patient
to focus awareness on the future so that the natural process
of Gestalt formation will take place.

10. _____   The goal of <u>Reichian biofunctional therapy</u> is accurate dream
analysis.

<u>Fill in the Blanks</u>

11. P_____ therapy holds that neurosis is caused by
rejection of the child by the parents.

12. G_____ therapy uses the social dimension as the pre-
dominant agent of c_____.

13. Encounter groups tend to be more concerned with adding something
p_____ to people's lives rather than with
removing something n_____.

14. Perhaps the most highly o_____ of all therapies is <u>est</u>.

15. T_____ a_____ holds that
behavior at any given time is dominated by one of three ego states: the
parent, the adult, or the child.

16. S_____ therapy defines the source of the emotional
problem as being biological in nature, and attempts to treat the problem
through some biological means such as d_____.

17. A widely used behavior therapy technique that was originally created for
the treatment of phobias is s_____ d_____.

18. C_____ therapists point out to their patients faulty
t_____ and confusion with regard to v_____
judgments.

19. A useful guideline to remember when choosing a therapy is that the
therapy should be suited to the p_____.

20. The risks of successful therapy extend to f_____
m_____ and f_____ as well as to the
person in therapy.

Answers and Question Numbers in REVIEW QUESTIONS sections of chapter.

1. True (1)

2. False (2)

3. True (4)

4. True (13)

5. True (14)

6. False (15)

7. True (16)

8. True (18)

9. False (20)

10. False (22)

11. Primal (23)

12. Group, change (25)

13. positive, negative (27)

14. organized (28)

15. Transactional analysis (29)

16. Somatic, drugs (34)

17. systematic desensitization (38)

18. Cognitive, thinking, value (40)

19. problem (41)

20. family members, friends (45)

Chapter
ELEVEN

Life Decisions and Life Goals

CHAPTER TERMS AND CONCEPTS

The following terms and concepts are considered essential to an understanding of the material presented in Chapter 11, "Life Decisions and Life Goals."

1. goal-related values and strengths
2. goal measurability
3. goal deadlines
4. long-range goals
5. short-term goals
6. goal priorities
7. goal-setting for success
8. goal expectations
9. related goals
10. enjoyable goals
11. goal-setting process
12. goal change
13. career change
14. retirement
15. retirement provisions
16. decision-making
17. satisfying decisions
18. steps to decision-making
19. value priorities
20. reviewing decisions

BEHAVIORAL OBJECTIVES

After reading and reflecting on the material presented in Chapter 11, "Life Decisions and Life Goals," you should be able to:

1. define the relationship between short-term and long-range goals;

2. define the relationship between decision-making and goal-setting;

3. apply successful goal-setting criteria to your own goals;

4. apply the seven steps in effective decision-making to your own life decisions;

5. establish a list of priorities.

SEARCH FOR MEANING

Respond to the following statements and questions after locating the information in Chapter 11.

1. What criteria are important when formulating our life goals? _____

_____

_____

_____

_____

_____

2. How is it possible to know when we have reached one of our life goals?

_____

_____

_____

_____

_____

3. Explain why it is important to set deadlines for achieving our life goals:

_____

_____

_____

_____

4. Give four examples of long-range goals:

    a. _____

    b. _____

    c. _____

    d. _____

5. Describe the relationship between long-range goals and short-term goals:

_____

_____

_____

_____

_____

6. Explain the importance of goal priorities. List some of your goal priori-
    ties as examples:

_____

_____

_____

_____

_____

7. Describe the main consideration when engaged in early goal-setting:

_____

_____

_____

_____

_____

8. What caution is warranted when setting goals of achieving recognition and
    appreciation from others?

_____

_____

_____

9. How can we look at the failure to reach a particular goal in a positive
    way?

_____

_____

_____

_____

10. List some major considerations when establishing long-range goal

priorities: _____

_____

_____

_____

_____

11. The goal-setting process is: _____

_____

_____

12. What assumptions can we make about people who change their goals later in life?

_____

_____

_____

_____

13. List reasons why a person may decide to change a career after many years:

_____

_____

_____

_____

_____

14. Describe how the concept of retirement is beginning to change in our society:

_____

_____

_____

_____

_____

15. List three important considerations before retirement:

a. _____

b. _____

c. _____

16. List at least four characteristics of effective decision-making:

a. _____

b. _____

c. _____

d. _____

e. _____

17. Describe the importance of our needs, values, and goals as they relate to decision-making:

_____

_____

_____

_____

_____

_____

18. List the steps to effective decision-making in proper order:

_____

_____

_____

_____

_____

19. Describe the information that should be given the most weight when preparing to make a decision:

_____

_____

_____

_____

_____

_____

20. What process continues after we have made an important decision? _____

_____

_____

_____

PERSONAL SYNTHESIS

    Contrary to what some people believe, success in life seldom happens
through luck. Most success stories result from carefully planned goals and
carefully made decisions. Reflect a moment on some of your goals and the
decisions you may have to make to reach these goals.

    Using as many terms and concepts as you can, write what you believe may
become your success story.

_____

_____

_____

_____

_____

_____

_____

_____

_____

_____

_____

_____

_____

_____

_____

_____

_____

_____

_____

_____

_____

_____

_____

_____

_____

_____

_____

_____

_____

_____

_____

_____

_____

_____

SELF QUIZ

True or False

1. _____ The advice of other successful people is the most important factor in formulating life goals.

2. _____ Completing a term paper is a good example of a short-term goal.

3. _____ Goal priorities help us establish a timetable for goal completion.

4. _____ The most rewarding goals are those wherein we expect to achieve recognition and appreciation from others.

5. _____ Failure to achieve a life goal usually results in low self-esteem.

6. _____ When establishing goal priorities, our most important goals should always be first.

7. _____ When we change goals later in life it may mean our values and interests have changed.

8. _____ To change a career later in life may be viewed as one of our greatest life decisions.

9. _____ The major concern of retirees should be financial security.

10. _____ Value priorities are very important considerations when making life decisions.

Fill in the Blanks

11. We can more easily know when one of our goals has been achieved if it is stated in _____ terms.

12. _____ help us more readily achieve our goals.

13. _____ _____ are those that we hope to achieve in the distant future.

14. _____ is a key factor in early goal-setting.

15. The _____ _____ need never be completed.

16. _____ is defined as the institutional separation of an individual from his or her occupational position.

17. Effective decision-making results from a _____ _____.

18. When making a personally satisfying decision, it is most important to con-
    sider our _____ and _____.

19. The first step in the decision-making process is _____ the
    _____.

20. The last step in the decision-making process is _____ the
    _____.

Answers and Question Numbers in REVIEW QUESTIONS section of chapter.

1. False (3, 4)   11. measurable (5)

2. True (9)   12. deadlines (6)

3. True (10, 11)   13. long-range goals (8)

4. False (15)   14. success (11)

5. False (16)   15. goal-setting process (18)

6. False (14, 17)   16. retirement (22)

7. True (19, 20)   17. step-by-step process (24, 28)

8. True (21)   18. needs, values (27)

9. False (23)   19. identifying, circumstance (28)

10. True (29)   20. reviewing, decision (33)

PART FOUR GROWTH THROUGH INTERACTION

Chapter
TWELVE

Intimacy

CHAPTER TERMS AND CONCEPTS

The following terms and concepts are considered essential to an understanding of the material presented in Chapter 12, "Intimacy."

1. physical intimacy
2. therapeutic touch
3. emotional intimacy
4. sexual intimacy
5. healthy relationships
6. the family
7. maternal and infant love
8. peer love

9. heterosexual love
10. paternal love

11. cohabitation
12. open marriage
13. convenience, privacy, mobility
14. the "giant shock absorber"
15. stress and intimacy
16. social loneliness
17. emotional loneliness
18. loneliness and depression, and suicide
19. existential loneliness
20. romantic love

BEHAVIORAL OBJECTIVES

After reading and reflecting on the material presented in Chapter 12, "Intimacy," you should be able to:

1. define the various aspects of intimacy;

2. describe the conditions for achieving satisfying intimacy;

3. trace the development of our capacity for intimacy in terms of Harlow's types of love;

4. describe the alternatives to marriage;

5. give examples of the factors inhibiting the achievement of satisfying intimacy;

131

6.   describe the effects of loneliness on our capacity for intimacy;

7.   describe the concept of romantic love as it relates to the development of satisfying relationships.

SEARCH FOR MEANING

Respond to the following statements or questions after locating appropriate information as it appears in Chapter 12.

1.   What are some of the taboos that surround touching? _____

_____

_____

_____

Why is physical intimacy important: _____

_____

_____

2.   Describe the significance of touch as viewed by Krieger, Peper, and Ancoli:

_____

_____

_____

_____

3.   Describe the conditions for emotional intimacy: _____

_____

_____

_____

4.   What is the relationship between emotional intimacy and sexual intimacy?

_____

_____

_____

_____

5. List the three characteristics of an emotionally healthy relationship:

a. _____

b. _____

c. _____

6. Who are the greatest providers of intimate contact during childhood?

_____

_____

7. Describe the relationship between mother and infant in terms of Harlow's types of love:

_____

_____

_____

8. What is the importance of peer-love on our development? _____

_____

_____

_____

_____

9. How does the family provide for the development of heterosexual love?

_____

_____

_____

_____

_____

_____

10. Describe the function of paternal love: _____

_____

_____

_____

11. What influence has Rimmer's <u>The Harrad Experiment</u> probably had on our
     society?

     _____

     _____

     _____

     _____

     _____

12. Define "Open Marriage" as proposed by Nena and George O'Neill: _____

     _____

     _____

     _____

     _____

     _____

13. List the three cherished freedoms that Keyes suggests may limit our
     chances for intimacy:

     a. _____

     b. _____

     c. _____

14. Explain the use of the concept "giant shock absorber" of society:

     _____

     _____

     _____

     _____

15. How does stress affect our capacity for intimacy? _____

     _____

     _____

     _____

     _____

16. What are the conditions surrounding social loneliness? _____

_____

_____

_____

_____

17. What factors contribute to emotional loneliness? _____

_____

_____

_____

_____

18. What do researchers such as Haven, Jacobs, and Lowenthal say about lone-
    liness?

_____

_____

_____

_____

19. What are the potential outcomes of existential loneliness? _____

_____

_____

_____

_____

20. What effect has the concept of romantic love had on our search for satis-
    fying intimacy?

_____

_____

_____

_____

_____

PERSONAL SYNTHESIS

    Our need for a satisfying intimate relationship is forever present. Concern for finding, maintaining, and developing intimacy occupies much of our waking time. Reflect for a moment on some of the thoughts and feelings that you experienced regarding your own need for intimacy while reading this chapter.

    Using as many terms and concepts from Chapter 12 as you can, assess the development of your own capacity for intimacy and assess the quality of your present intimate relationship(s).

_____

_____

_____

_____

_____

_____

_____

_____

_____

_____

_____

_____

_____

_____

_____

_____

_____

_____

_____

SELF QUIZ

True or False

1. _____ Our highest level of intimacy is physical intimacy.

2. _____ Contrary to religious belief, sex is a necessity for everyone.

3. _____ The physical parallel to emotional intimacy is sexual intimacy.

4. _____ Playmates of the same sex are our greatest providers of intimate contact during childhood.

5. _____ Heterosexual love emerges around puberty and develops from observing other family members.

6. _____ Maternal love serves mainly as a protective system for the child from birth to puberty.

7. _____ "Open Marriage" is the term given to the concept of physical and emotional relationships outside the traditional form of marriage.

8. _____ The church has been termed the "giant shock absorber" of society.

9. _____ Women working outside the home has been one of the major contributors to society's decreased capacity for intimacy.

10. _____ Lowenthal, Haven, and Jacobs indicate that there is a direct correlation between suicide and loneliness.

Fill in the Blanks

11. According to Krieger, Peper, and Ancoli, the act of touching has greater power than believed previously. They report that there is evidence that touch has _____ _____ value.

12. The healthy, emotionally intimate relationship is characterized by _____, _____, and _____.

13. _____ and _____ are the types of intimacy described by Harlow that define the relationship between a mother and child.

14. _____ is the type of love that has long-range effects on our personal/social adjustment.

15. Rimmer's novel, The Harrad Experiment, probably has had some influence on the increasing social practice of _____.

16. Keyes suggests that three of our cherished freedoms have had an impact on our quality of intimacy. These freedoms are _____, _____, and _____.

17. _____ is the term given to the state of lacking a supportive social group.

18. Lacking an intimate relationship with one significant other often results in _____ _____.

19. _____ _____ is the state of experiencing solitude to reflect on the condition of one's life.

20. _____ _____ is an idealized set of expectations used to judge the quality of a love relationship.

Answers and Question Numbers in REVIEW QUESTIONS section of chapter.

1. False (1, 2)

2. False (4)

3. True (6)

4. False (11)

5. True (14)

6. False (11)

7. True (18)

8. False (23)

9. False (26)

10. True (29)

11. therapeutic healing (3)

12. accessibility, naturalness, non-possessiveness (7)

13. maternal love, infant love (12)

14. peer love (13)

15. cohabitation (16, 17)

16. convenience, mobility, privacy (20, 21, 23)

17. Social loneliness (27)

18. emotional loneliness (28)

19. Existential loneliness (30)

20. Romantic love (31, 32, 33)

Chapter
THIRTEEN

Communication

CHAPTER TERMS AND CONCEPTS

The following terms and concepts are considered essential to an understanding of the material presented in Chapter 13, "Communication."

1. communication
2. The Awareness Wheel
3. feeling statements
4. responsible communication
5. indirect statements
6. misused questions
7. types of questions
8. communication and self-concept
9. listening
10. deceptive listening
11. "listening with the third ear"
12. Shared Meaning Process
13. styles of communication
14. influencing change
15. tentative communication
16. nonverbal communication
17. "window to the soul"
18. facial expressions
19. assertive communication
20. congruent communication

BEHAVIORAL OBJECTIVES

After reading and reflecting on the material presented in Chapter 13,
"Communication," you should be able to:

1. identify the components of effective communication;

2. describe the relationship among the components of communication;

3. differentiate between thinking and feeling statements;

4. give examples of assertive communication;

5. describe the process of active listening;

6. describe the importance of nonverbal communication.

SEARCH FOR MEANING

Respond to the following statements and questions after locating the appropriate information as it appears in Chapter 13.

1. Communication is defined as: _____

    _____

    _____

2. Describe the usefulness of each dimension of The Awareness Wheel:

    a. _____

    b. _____

    c. _____

    d. _____

    e. _____

3. List five words that accurately describe our feelings:

    a. _____

    b. _____

    c. _____

    d. _____

    e. _____

4. What are the typical results when we assume that we know what someone is thinking and/or feeling?

    _____

    _____

    _____

5. Give three examples of indirect statements:

    a. _____

    _____

    b. _____

    _____

c. _____

_____

What is the intention of the sender in each example?

a. _____

b. _____

c. _____

6. What does the statement, "Questions are the most indirect form of communication." mean?

_____

_____

_____

_____

_____

_____

7. Give an example that you may have used for each of the following types of questions:

a. "Got'cha" question: _____

_____

_____

b. Punitive question: _____

_____

_____

c. Imperative question: _____

_____

_____

d. Screened question: _____

_____

_____

e. Co-optive question: _____

_____

_____

8. What effect does our self-concept have on our ability to communicate?

_____

_____

_____

_____

_____

9. Define the process of listening: _____

_____

_____

_____

_____

_____

10. Define "deceptive listening": _____

_____

_____

_____

_____

11. What does Reik mean by "listening with the third ear"? _____

_____

_____

_____

_____

12. Describe the usefulness of the "shared meaning process." _____

_____

_____

_____

_____

_____

_____

_____

13. When is it appropriate to use the style of communication termed "chit chat"?

_____

_____

_____

14. List five communication behaviors designed to influence change in a situation:

a. _____

b. _____

c. _____

d. _____

e. _____

15. Describe the usefulness of the tentative style of communication:

_____

_____

_____

_____

16. List several ways that non-verbal communication contributes to the communication process:

a. _____

b. _____

c. _____

d. _____

17. The eye is often referred to as "the window to the soul." What is the meaning of this reference?

_____

_____

_____

_____

18. Describe the importance of the face as a source of nonverbal communication:

_____

_____

_____

_____

_____

_____

List 10 different expressions communicated by the face:

a. _____   f. _____

b. _____   g. _____

c. _____   h. _____

d. _____   i. _____

e. _____   j. _____

19. Describe the difference between <u>aggressive communication</u> and <u>assertive communication</u>:

_____

_____

_____

_____

_____

_____

_____

Give three examples of <u>aggressive</u> communication:

a. _____

b. _____

c. _____

Give an <u>assertive</u> example for each of the above:

a. _____

b. _____

c. _____

20. Describe how the term <u>congruence</u> applies to effective communication:

_____

_____

_____

_____

_____

_____

_____

_____

PERSONAL SYNTHESIS

To effectively communicate is the personal responsibility of each of us. Reflect for a moment on what you have learned while reading this chapter.

Using as many terms and concepts from Chapter 13 as you can, (1) assess your present <u>abilities</u> and <u>liabilities</u> in effectively communicating and listening, (2) identify the areas of communication which you think you might want to <u>improve</u> upon, and (3) describe some strategies for working on these desired changes:

(1) _____

_____

_____

_____

(2)

(3)

SELF QUIZ

True or False

1. _____ When we express our <u>feelings</u>, they are either dishonest or honest.

2. _____ To assume that you know what another person is feeling or thinking is to demonstrate <u>irresponsible</u> <u>behavior</u>.

3. _____ The <u>question</u> is one of the most abused forms of communication.

4. _____ Our <u>self-concept</u> has little to do with our ability to communicate effectively.

5. _____ When we "listen with the third ear," we are listening for the <u>thoughts</u> and <u>key words</u> in the message.

6. _____ We are using the style of communication designed to <u>influence change</u> when we attempt to <u>persuade</u> someone to adopt our views.

7. _____ The <u>accommodating</u> style of communication is most effective when we are dealing with a <u>sensitive relationship</u> issue.

8. _____ The <u>ear</u> is often referred to as "the window to the soul."

9. _____ <u>Facial expressions</u> are the greatest multicultural means of expressing feeling.

10. _____ Communication with understanding as the goal is more likely to be effective when all aspects are <u>congruent</u>.

Fill in the Blanks

11. The process of sending and receiving messages with understanding is called _____.

12. The model in Chapter 13 which helps us learn to convey a more accurate message is called The _____ _____.

13. People often use _____ statements when their actual intention is to confuse others.

14. "Didn't I see you the other night with the boss at Joe's Lounge?" is an example of the _____ _____.

15. _____ is the process of searching for understanding and meaning in the message.

16. We are practicing _____ listening when we are pretending to listen but are actually thinking about something else.

17. The _____ _____
    _____ is one way we can check on the listener's
    understanding of our important message.

18. _____ is a style of communication that we may
    use to help make the time pass more quickly.

19. We are communicating _____ when we communicate
    all or part of a message without spoken words.

20. "I am really feeling hurt as a result of how you are treating me." is an
    example of _____ communication.

Answers and Question Numbers in REVIEW QUESTIONS section of chapter.

1. True (4, 5, 6, 7)   11. communication (1)

2. True (8)   12. Awareness Wheel (3)

3. True (10, 12)   13. indirect (9, 13, 14)

4. False (15, 16)   14. got'cha question (10, 12)

5. False (19)   15. listening (17)

6. True (23)   16. deceptive (18)

7. False (24)   17. shared meaning process (20, 21)

8. False (28, 29)   18. chit chat (22)

9. True (30)   19. non-verbally (25, 26, 27)

10. True (32)   20. assertive (11)

Chapter
FOURTEEN

The Individual and the Group

CHAPTER TERMS AND CONCEPTS

The following terms and concepts are considered essential to an understanding of the material in Chapter 14, "The Individual and the Group."

1. leadership
2. shared leadership
3. managers vs. leaders
4. designated leaders
5. power

6. referent power
7. expert power
8. legitimate power
9. reward power
10. coercive power

11. bureaucratic/pyramidal value system
12. Theory X and Theory Y
13. humanistic/democratic value system
14. Herzberg's Theory of Motivation
15. Likert's Autocratic/Democratic Continuum
16. effective leadership
17. maturity and situational leadership
18. integrative leadership
19. skills
20. learned leader vs. learning leader

BEHAVIORAL OBJECTIVES

After reading and reflecting on the material presented in Chapter 14, "The Individual and the Group," you should be able to:

1. define effective leadership as it relates to different organizational situations;

2. describe the relationship between leadership and management;

3. describe the different uses of power as it relates to leadership;

4. describe and identify the different leadership styles;

5. assess your own leadership style;

6. diagnose the organizational dynamics of groups and organizations to which you belong or have belonged.

SEARCH FOR MEANING

Complete the following statements after locating the appropriate information as it appears in Chapter 14.

1. Define leadership: _____

    _____

    _____

    _____

2. What is meant by shared leadership? _____

    _____

    _____

    _____

3. Describe the differences and similarities between managers and leaders:

    _____

    _____

    _____

    _____

    _____

    _____

    _____

4. Many organizations have designated leaders. In what ways are these leaders chosen?

    _____

    _____

    _____

    _____

5. Define the term power as it applies to effective leadership: _____

_____

_____

_____

_____

6. An important type of power demonstrated by people such as Abraham Lincoln
   and John F. Kennedy is termed _____.
   Define this type of power:

_____

_____

_____

_____

7. Define expert power: _____

_____

_____

_____

8. What type of leaders have legitimate power? _____

_____

_____

_____

9. Give an example of reward power: _____

_____

_____

_____

10. A common use of power is referred to as coercive power. Define coercive
    power, and give examples:

_____

_____

_____

_____

_____

_____

11. Elton <u>Mayo</u> has made a contribution to the study of leadership and groups. What were the findings from his <u>Hawthorne Studies</u>?

_____

_____

_____

_____

_____

_____

_____

_____

12. Describe the differences between <u>McGregor's</u> <u>Theory X</u> <u>and</u> <u>Theory Y</u>:

Theory X _____

_____

_____

_____

Theory Y _____

_____

_____

_____

13. What is the <u>humanistic/democratic value system</u>? _____

_____

_____

_____

14. List Herzberg's motivating factors: _____

_____

_____

_____

_____

15. Name and describe <u>Rensis Likert's</u> four leadership style systems:

a. System I _____: _____

_____

_____

_____

_____

b. System II _____: _____

_____

_____

_____

_____

c. System III _____: _____

_____

_____

_____

_____

d. System IV _____: _____

_____

_____

_____

_____

_____

16. What does the text mean when it refers to <u>effective</u> <u>leadership</u>?

_____

_____

_____

_____

_____

_____

17. Describe the <u>maturity</u> component of Hersey and Blanchard's Situational Leadership Theory:

_____

_____

_____

_____

_____

18. Define <u>integrative leadership style</u>: _____

_____

_____

_____

_____

_____

19. List several important <u>diagnostic</u> <u>skills</u> characteristic of the effective leader:

a. _____

b. _____

c. _____

d. _____

20. What is the difference between a <u>learned</u> <u>leader</u> and a <u>learning</u> <u>leader</u>?

_____

_____

_____

_____

_____

_____

_____

Which one is most effective as a leader? _____

_____

PERSONAL SYNTHESIS

At some point in our lives, each of us thinks about what it would be like
to be a boss, leader, manager, president, or chairperson of some organization.
As a college student, you may hope that your college training someday will
result in a leadership position.

Using as many terms and concepts from Chapter 14 as you can, describe the
style of leadership you will hope to use if the opportunity comes for you to
assume leadership responsibilities.

_____

_____

_____

_____

_____

_____

_____

_____

_____

_____

_____

SELF QUIZ

True or False

1. _____ Leadership is defined as getting other people to do what you want them to do at all cost.

2. _____ The type of leadership that provides for all members of an organization to make significant contributions to the achievement of the organization's goals is called shared leadership.

3. _____ Power is defined as the ability to require a particular behavior of other group members.

4. _____ A person who influences others by use of "charisma" is said to have reward power.

5. _____ When someone has the power to withhold your paycheck or fire you, that person has coercive power.

6. _____ Elton Mayo's Hawthorne's Studies showed that people are motivated by numerous fringe benefits.

7. _____ The belief that most people dislike work and therefore must be closely watched and coerced is an assumption of McGregor's Theory Y.

8. _____ Encouraging others to share in the organization's decision-making process is a characteristic of the humanistic/democratic value system.

9. _____ Rensis Likert believes that most people are dictatorial-type leaders who enjoy telling others what to do.

10. _____ The most effective leader is one who is termed a learned leader.

Fill in the Blanks

11. Abraham Zaleznik believes that _____ and _____ differ in motivation, personal history, and how they think and act.

12. _____ leaders are usually chosen by appointment or by election.

13. _____ _____ is the influence that someone holds by possessing special knowledge needed by others.

14. A designated leader usually has _____ power.

15. When you have the ability to give something to someone that they want for doing what you want, you have _____ power.

16. Herzberg's Motivating Factors consist of achievement, _____, work itself, _____ and _____.

17. _____ leadership is characterized by an appropriate personality and behavior conducive to the achievement of the individual's and organization's goals.

18. Hersey's and Blanchard's Situational Leadership Theory is based on the belief that the effectiveness of a particular leadership style depends on the level of _____ of the group members and the situation.

19. An _____ leadership style is one that is able to adapt to the individual's needs and the needs of the organization.

20. Fritz Roethlisberger suggests three skill areas for leadership effectiveness: (1) _____ and the realization of our impact on others, (2) the skills of being able to _____ a situation, and (3) the skills of helping _____ and _____ to grow and develop.

Answers and Question Numbers in REVIEW QUESTIONS section of chapter.

 1. False (1)   11. managers, leaders (5)

 2. True (2)   12. Designated (7, 8)

 3. True (8, 9, 10)   13. Expert power (10)

 4. False (9)   14. legitimate (8, 9, 10)

 5. True (8, 9, 10)   15. reward (8, 9, 10)

 6. False (11)   16. recognition, responsibility, professional growth (16)

 7. False (12)   17. Effective (19, 28)

 8. True (14)   18. maturity (20)

 9. False (17)   19. integrative (21)

10. False (26)   20. self-awareness, diagnose, oneself, others (25, 27)

†